JEF

YURIY TARNAWSKY

ACADEME GROVE
INTERVIEWS 2017-2023

JEF

2025

Cover Art & Design by Norman Conquest

ISBN 1-884097-08-1

ISBN-13 978-1-884097-08-9

ISSN 1084-547X

This is volume 105 of the Journal of Experimental Fiction

JEF Books/Depth Charge Publishing

Arlington Heights, Illinois

JEF Books/Depth Charge Publishing

"The Foremost in Innovative Fiction"

Experimentalfiction.com

TABLE OF CONTENTS

TO THE READER

This book contains all eleven interviews conducted with me during the years 2017-2023, some in the original English, others in my own translation from the Ukrainian. I would like to extend my thanks to the interviewers for their effort and interest in my work, and to invite you, dear reader, if you will ever be, to take these strolls through the virtual grove of ancient Academus I took with others, which, I hope, you will find informative and rewarding.

—Yuriy Tarnawsky

INTERVIEW WITH VOLODYMYR BILYK

Talking with Ukrainian writers is harder than you think. You need to ask more questions than usual and you need to explain a lot for the reader. Mainly because no one really knows a thing about Ukrainian literature and its rather unique place in worlds culture. It's complicated, strange and terrible. It lays where Chtulhu sleeps and acts like an idiot savant. It's irritating at best and utterly annoying at worst. Also – Kick the chair. Don't forget to breathe. Down with that boring stuff.

Yuriy Tarnawsky is the guy who writes. Long and short stuff. In English and Ukrainian. You probably heard of him once or twice or more. He wrote Three Blondes and Death *and some other stuff. And if you want me to retell his biography – ask me to write an article in the comments.*

I find it funny trying to start an interview naturally. The more I do interviews, it starts to look less like attempting to clear one set of things and set straight the other and more like going into the realms of meta and strolling around aimlessly. Talking about art is double funny because it makes no sense. For real. It's just an illusion – another version – parallel reality. It's just what it is.

Yuriy Tarnawsky

This interview was started in late 2015, dragged on through 2016 and finally ended in 2017. Not that it was that long. It's more like – "your truly needs to sustain himself and this thing is not helping." But you don't need to know that.

So – here's my long gestating interview with YT, sometime in January-February. Enjoy.

VB: Every time I start preparing myself for an interview, I think "what do I want to achieve with it?" And every time I don't know how to answer. I fail to understand why I'm doing this. It's a fascinating moment. What do you feel when someone asks you to do an interview? Do you have this indescribable power? The moment after you receive a message? Or is it inner "Roger Daltrey" screaming, "Yeah!" and imaginary sunglasses cover your eyes?

YT: Sort of neither. It's probably the scientist inside, or, better still, outside me who wants to get down to brass tacks and lay out before the world what it is I'm all about as a writer. I never take on my literary persona when I'm answering questions but become a dispassionate observer looking from some distance on the subject that is me and am ready to talk about it and dissect it to the core. I think it was no coincidence that I studied engineering and then generative linguistics rather than literature. The literary part of me is very private and I have built up this scientific wall around me to

2

protect it. As you know, I also avoid bringing in autobiographical data into my writing, but turn to imagination to bounce off of it (the data).

Now.

What do you think about interviews as an art form? Does it help you to rethink and re-express the ideas you've expressed in your works? Or is it just another way to try your artistic M.O. in conversation?

As I have just intimated, I don't look at it as an art form but rather as a scientific or scholarly undertaking and turn to the analytic part of me. JEF Books has just brought out my book of "selected essays and interviews" *Claim to Oblivion.* The interviews in it are very much like the essays—I analyze and explain what my works are about. The Ukrainian-language book of essays and interviews *Kvity khvoromu (Flowers for the Patient)* is also like that. In fact, in it I openly say that the interviews are articles in the form of dialogues.

Is it necessary for an artist to give interviews? In an existential sense – to express something the other way. Can it be harmful and traumatizing at some point? Why?

No, it's not necessary at all. It depends on what you want to do. At this time at least, I personally like to do interviews, probably

Yuriy Tarnawsky

because of my pretty hermetic writing, to explain what it is I'm trying to do. Again, it's the scientist part of me that does it, that has been activated by the request for an interview. As a militant modernist, I try to change the world (art, literature) through my writing and feel that speaking openly about what I try to do will help me in my task.

As you know, I feel that postmodernism is part of modernism, its third phase, and that it bears many of the important features of classical modernism, except that some commercial writers, such as Umberto Eco, have managed to sneak into it and go for a ride.

Interviews can offer a possibility to enrich the reading experience but there's also a probability to spoil it – what do you think about those little things that make difference? What do you think about going too far in conversation and giving away too much?

Yes, I do think that you can spoil your writing by talking to much about it, "giving away" something important (sacred). So, you have to be careful what you say. Say only what should be said and don't destroy what you've built up.

How about misleading? Or misinterpreting yourself?

Well, yes, that's dangerous too. You may inadvertently misrepresent yourself, so you've got to be careful. On the other

4

hand, there are some who do it deliberately, treat it as part of their art. Dali was definitely like that. And it had served him well. But I don't do that. I didn't go into literature to become famous or rich, but to speak of what ails/excites me. So, that's why I approach an interview as a scientist.

Is it important to change gears and try it another way? Like not talking about anything important or interesting and just do it the way it goes – like a kind of jazz or comedy improv?

I 'm not interested in that. Maybe one day.... You've given me an idea....

What are the key elements that make interview worth reading, in your opinion? Is it useful information or just a glimpse of a real person behind the personae? Or is it the sacramental "something else?" (Or it depends on what is the practical purpose of a particular interview?)

It depends on what the interviewee does. It could be any one of those things. Now that you've got me rethinking along your lines, I begin to see how an interview could be a form of art in which you extend what you do in your writing.

What do you think about growing tendency of interviews turning into a clickbait?

If by "*clickbait*" you mean self-promotion—then yeah, most commercial artists use the interview to unabashedly self-promote. I'm not interested in doing it, unless you take my "scientific" explanation as self-promotion, which you can. But it's gentle promotion, "classy" I'd call it.

February 19, 2016

Can you describe your more or less ordinary\standard writing session? How do you prepare yourself? How do you start? Is there any order of things you do – first and last? Is it important to have some kind of discipline? Do you have any special ways of putting yourself in the mood for the act?

The standard over the years has been that it has varied, and has varied not only over a period of time, but at times from book to book. I have more or less settled right now on an accepted *modus operandi* of just sitting down at the computer and pounding out language strings, but in the past I would sometimes develop a novel routine as I started working on a new book—the kind of paper and pen I'd use, when I would write, what I would be reading or listening to at that time (when I wasn't writing), and so on, which I'd associate with what I was writing and which would help me move along.

Before we had computers, I'd write the text out in longhand, correct it a few times, and then type it up, correct it again, and type it up once more. Then after the arrival of computers, I'd always start out with longhand text and then do extensive rewriting on the computer. This went on for a long time. But lately my handwriting has gotten so bad, I can barely read it, so I almost always do the original text on the computer and then edit/rewrite it on the computer.

I like to start out in the morning, fresh, preferably on an empty stomach, work for 2-3 hours (more I can't do, as my mind starts wondering off), and take a break. Then in the afternoon, I'd do the editing, perhaps 2-4 hours; editing is easier than composing from scratch. In the past, I'd do my writing and then forget about it during the rest of the day. But a while back (20-30 years ago?) I learned that the best way was to think about what I was wring all the time, so that I'd have a lot of problems solved before sitting down at the computer, and then just pound it out. I find this to be the most effective way—it takes much less time at the keyboard. But there are still variations dependent on what I'm working on. Prose and poetry, for instance, are different—I might jot down poetry on paper and then type it up. You can compose a page of poetry in your head, but you can't do it with prose. In short—I have no standard procedure, except that I try to be connected to what I'm working on day and night. Sleep is wonderful for composing.

Yuriy Tarnawsky

Since you've been around for a long time I want to ask you this stupid thing: are there any technical differences in the way you did the writing back in the 50's/60's (and so on) and now?

Not a stupid question at all, very to the point. The advent of computers has changed a writer's (my own) life tremendously. Being able to see text neatly typed up on the screen and redo it there is a tremendous aid. We, I at least, write much, much faster now. I'd estimate that it's about three times faster to write now for me than it was before computers. And I think the quality is better too. You have a better view (sort of a bird's- eye view) of what you're doing and can spot problems much more easily and fix them more easily too.

What about revisions? Do you revisit the finished text in order to fix it or refit something? Or you just get over it?

As I said earlier, I edit what I write shortly after writing it down. That's the first rewrite. After composing a chunk, I may do the next rewriting—pulling the sub-chunks together, making them fit better. I might do it a number of times, depending on how difficult the text is. And when the whole text is done, I start a new rewriting process, and may repeat it a number of times, depending on how difficult the text is. It's all very organic, dependent on the work and my state of mind.

What do you think about overwriting for the thing – doing too much – to the point of sheer abundance? Do you make use of leftover materials? Do you repurpose them or they "perish in flames?"

Personally, I don't have this problem. That is, I'm not aware of it. I usually put down on paper what I need and there's no leftover. But, of course, there are things I abandon, and I may use some of them in other works. Not use pieces of them, but the abandoned work may lead me to a completely new one which works this time.

How about scrapped ideas? Have you ever toyed with some concept, but it never moved further, "thinking about it" but it still "hurts," and you want to try it somehow but you just can't figure out the way of doing it?

Yes, I did, as I've just, mentioned. In fact, I've made good use of this problem/technique in the past. Some ideas that didn't pan out, all of a sudden open out wonderful new possibilities before you. I think an artist-writer (a noncommercial writer) has essentially one great mother lode of topics/ideas he wants to write about, and everything he does is part of a whole. So, his oeuvre maybe viewed as one huge book. And these little abandoned pieces are part of this big whole and will be useful later.

Yuriy Tarnawsky

Have you ever thought about doing a "parallel universe" version of the text? Or a mirror reflection" variation?

No, I haven't. It's a writing technique, I guess, and I haven't tried it. Right now, I don't seem to have a need for it somehow.

There's this lousy Beckett quote – it goes something like "Try – fail – try again – fail better" – isn't it plain B&W hypocrite? I think the concept behind it deserves to be mocked on every occasion as severe misleading of the whole concept of creative act. What do you think?

Black-and-white hypocrisy? I don't see it like that. The quote must be from *The Unnamable*, and if not, then from one of his other works which are part of his one huge book. (He's an excellent example of the artist-writer. Eco died today. *De mortuis nihil nisi bene*, but I can't refrain from saying, he certainly wasn't one.) It probably refers to living rather than writing, or if it does refer to writing, then writing as part of living. But creating is hard work, and you've got to try again, and again, and again, until you succeed, if you want to succeed.

Sometime in November, 2016
Let's move ab ovo—what was the moment when you understood that writing expresses you fully and you decided to fully devote yourself to it?

It took me a while. My writing career started out as a reader. I longed to live in an imaginary world and looked for it in books. When books ran out, I started writing. This was around 1950 in the DP camp in Neu Ulm, Germany, and books were scarce there. What I wrote then was fiction, and it was pure crap, and led to nothing.

After I came to the US in 1952, books became plentiful, and I had no urge to write, didn't dare to do it, feeling I was a mere mortal, and writers were gods or demigods at least. But as I grew older, feelings began to stir in me like earth worms in the soil in springtime, and I began to dabble in poetry—getting my feelings out, mostly about the absurdity of life which I began to notice. But I still didn't think of myself as a writer but a private "feelings recorder."

Gradually though, I began to feel brave enough to think I might try submitting something for publication, and so in 1953 I had my first poem published in the Ukrainian newspaper *Svoboda* which came out in New Jersey, and, starting in 1954, a few short prose pieces in the newspaper *Contemporary Ukraine* which came out in Munich. In 1955 I began putting together a book of poems, which ultimately came out in 1956 under the title *Zhyttja v misti (Life in the City)*, working at the same time on fiction—short stories in English and a novel in Ukrainian. Nothing came out of the first effort, but an excerpt from the novel, which is called *Shljakhy*

(Roads), was published in 1956 and the whole novel in 1961. By then I was well on my way toward thinking of myself as a writer—*homo scribens*—not being aware of the misery that comes with this appellation—the constant struggle with the blank page and the craving for recognition which almost never reaches the desired level.

What was the catalyst? How did it come to fruition? And what was your primary motivation?

The primary catalyst was a search for an imaginary life, and then the need to express what I felt, a reaction to what life was doing to me. What helped me a lot was the fact that even though I was a small fish, the pond I swam in was small too—*kalabanja*, a puddle—the Ukrainian émigré society. There weren't that many young writers coming up, so getting published wasn't that hard. My only motivation, throughout my life as a writer, has been tackling the existential questions of the fear of death, alienation, and so forth. It was never a desire to make money or be famous. Writing for me is a purely existential act—I write, therefore I am.

How has your attitude toward writing changed through time? When did you start to shift from more traditional writing to more experimental? Has it come naturally, or was it your decision to change gears? Why did you do it? What were your guiding lights? Or was it a kind of an old-school journey into the unknown?

I was always a "do it my way" kind of a person (child) from the beginning. I taught myself alone to read and write, and formed letters in my own unique way. It was the same with literature. The poetry I wrote was free verse from the beginning. I don't think I knew much about free verse before coming to the US, and that may have been the reason why I didn't write any poetry while I lived in Germany. Ukrainian poetry was all traditional and I found it silly—why would anyone want to look for words which sounded the same at the end of lines? When I saw English and especially Spanish poetry written in free verse, that opened my eyes, and with it my desire to write poetry. Here I was able to write as I felt. *Life in the City* was considered revolutionary in Ukrainian literary circles, such that it broke with the attitude toward language, prevalent among Ukrainians, as something of necessity melodious, as well as with the traditional themes and forms. And so it was with fiction. I thought I wrote *Roads* in the standard fashion, but Ukrainian critics thought of it as an antinovel. In my English writing—fiction—I grew bolder. By then I was aware of the rules that traditional writers used and saw that, first, they didn't lead to anything interesting, and, second, that they were not inviolable. Breaking them, you could achieve all sort of interesting effects. So, it was this that drove me on. This attitude has stayed on with me until this day.

As to guiding lights—I was influenced primarily by Spanish and French poetry, modernism in general and Surrealist in particular, the philosophy of Existentialism, and modernist cinema. My favorite poet is Arthur Rimbaud; fiction writers, Gogol, Kleist, and Proust; and composer—J. S. Bach, especially as interpreted by Glenn Gould.

Can you say more about the circumstances under which you started writing fiction in English? Was it simply because there were not many Ukrainian readers? Or was it more of an aesthetic choice?

I was surrounded by English and used it a lot, so it seemed natural for me to write in it, that's all. I had no other, ulterior motives, certainly, nothing connected with gain.

What were your first American readers like? What were the initial reactions? When did you understand that you've found your readership?

My first books in English were published by Fiction Collective (FC), so my first readers were the kind of people who read FC books—people interested in innovative writing, mostly creative writing professors and college students. I realized I had found my literary home when I began to communicate with my FC author friends and to attend the AWP and &NOW conferences. The feeling was gratifying, akin to finding yourself on a cold winter night in a snug home, with a mug of hot tea and rum in your hand, next to a fireplace with a fire roaring inside it, while a storm rages outside.

What was the atmosphere surrounding you at that time? Aside from the diaspora —who were in your social group at that time?

Before I joined FC, it was the Ukrainian émigré society—some the older generation figures—Yuriy Lavrinenko, for instance, the literary critic who became my literary godfather—and my colleagues from the New York Group, the group of innovative Ukrainian émigré writers I helped to co-found, as well as artists who were close to the group, in particular Jurij Solovij, who did the lion's share of the artwork in the Group's publications.

What was the nature of their influence?

It wasn't influence as such, but simply friendship, a feeling they gave me that I wasn't alone. It's hard to charge against traditions on your own. You need to feel there's someone beside and behind you.

You have a rich background in computing and linguistics—was it the desire to expand upon theoretical concepts in a completely different direction that driven you into more experimental "parts unknown" in your writing?

Yuriy Tarnawsky

It wasn't a "desire" as such, but simply an inclination, which, I presume came partly from my personality—my always doing things in my own way—and partly from my technical background. The latter, I'm sure, made me see literature in a different way from the way people with nontechnical background see it. In describing my attitude to writing, I've been saying lately that for me, composing a literary work is similar (identical) to a mathematician proving a theorem—the goal is to do it as simply and elegantly as possible. The question whether it will be interesting to or easy on the reader never comes up.

What did the work on natural-language processing bring into your fiction writing?

It made me aware of the nature of language, its patterns and capabilities—how I could affect the reader by using it in various nonstandard ways.

Since you've worked with Artificial Intelligence, have you ever considered writing something fictional about artificial intelligence?

Sort of science fiction, you mean? Absolutely not. When I think about writing now, I still think only of those ponderous existential issues. That's what true literature is for me. To paraphrase Verlaine, everything else is commercial products for sale.

Do you remember that presumably Frank-Zappa quote "...dancing about architecture?" Since the concept of art is more or less considered to be "anything you want and nothing in particular," is it really important to talk about such things seriously? It often makes a kind of unintended comedy. Sometimes I read "Art of fiction" in Paris Review and it's so peacocky pathetic – it's more like "make yourself believe you said that for real" than "that's how the things really are." What do you think about such attempts to sort it out and remain reasonable?

I haven't followed Frank Zappa much, so I'm not acquainted with the quote. But I don't accept the idea that anything is art which has been espoused by many these days, stemming from those acts of insight and defiance by Marcel Duchamp in the early days of the last century. But Duchamp was an artist, as his "A Nude Descending a Staircase" so convincingly shows, and many of our contemporaries who claim to be aren't. Duchamp's bicycle wheel and urinal were art for an instant, when the viewer first saw them, but they ceased to be that thereafter and have now only historical value. (This is not true of his "Nude" and "Bride," which will remain works of art forever.) Modernism has taught us to strip the fake and unnecessary off works of art so as to reveal the real. Destruction must be followed by creation. Much of what we see these days doesn't even destroy, let enough create. It's cheating for the most part, neither more nor less.

Yuriy Tarnawsky

First published in Zouch Magazine & Miscellany, *June 17, 2017. Edited by Yuriy Tarnawsky. Volodymyr Bilyk is a Ukrainian poet and artist.*

INTERVIEW WITH ANNA PROCYK

There are not too many books which captivate the imagination so much that after the first paragraph you know that you have to read them at one sitting. This has been my experience with Yuriy Tarnawsky's latest novel Warm Arctic Nights. *From the author's dedication I sensed that this work would be somewhat more autobiographical than most novels tend to be. Therefore, I was most pleasantly surprised by the spirit of authenticity and freshness that pervades the novel's content. Naturally, I had to discuss the book with the author at the first opportunity. After the discussion and a few exchanges of notes we came up with the idea of an interview.*

AP: Approximately when did you get the idea to write this book? Was there anything in particular that prompted you to write the story of your childhood?

YT: The story of the first ten and a half years of my life that terminated in my leaving Ukraine, which I consider the most important in my biography, had been on my mind ever since I started thinking of myself as a writer. I felt certain that one day I would write it, but for a long time was reluctant to tackle the task. I felt instinctively it would be a difficult thing to do and that I wasn't yet up to it. Then some thirty years ago or so, I remember hearing on the radio an ad urging people to go on Caribbean cruises, extolling among their virtues the chance of enjoying "cool tropical nights" spent on the islands to be visited. I found the phrase to be a delightful oxymoron and immediately thought of its antonym "warm arctic nights," which I also immediately felt would be a great title for the story I was planning to write. It would neatly combine within itself the beauty and horror of those years of my childhood.

Impelled by the title, some time soon afterwards, I tried writing the book, but ran into serious difficulties. My fiction, with the lone exception of the novel *Meningitis*, is virtually totally devoid of autobiographical material and relies heavily on the ability of my imagination to dream up situations which optimally lend themselves to what I want to tell the reader. This is one reason I use so frequently dream scenes in my writing—unhampered by the laws of nature, I am able even more freely to mold the reader's mind. But in the case of my story, the biographical material, which was the seed of it, was so strong that I was unable to let my imagination run free. It kept getting in my way all the time and what I wanted to say just wouldn't come out. I set the novel aside and went back to it a while later, but was faced with the same difficulty. I tried this about half a dozen times more over the next twenty some years, and each time was faced with the same difficulty. In the end, perhaps five years ago, after trying to write the book once again and being unable to do it, I decided I had to give up on it. The topic was too difficult and I would never turn it into a book.

But this weighed heavy on my conscience—what kind of a writer was I if there was a topic which I was incapable of handling? I felt ashamed and considered myself inadequate—I would never be the writer I wanted to be.

But my conscience wouldn't leave me alone and deep inside I was still hoping I would one day write the book, and so in the fall of 2017, aware of my not inconsiderable age, I told myself that this was my last chance. I would either write the book then or would never be able to do it.

The ultimatum worked.

One thing that kept getting in my way of writing the book was shaping the narrative of the story. I kept trying the usual expository style and each time it wasn't coming out right. It was stiff and awkward and I wasn't able to let the narration flow. This time, in despair, I resorted to the principle I employ in the genre of the *mininovel* which I developed—write only what pleases you and leave out the rest. I asked myself how would I begin the story and answered—with the appearance of the room in which I was born. And so, I began the book with the question "How was the room?" and proceed answering it. The answer came easily, and so did the rest of the book, which I did in the same fashion, finishing it in six months.

Yuriy Tarnawsky

It was adopting this "interview" form that enabled me finally to write the novel.

Did you stick strictly to the autobiographical data? In other words, is it a work of fiction or an autobiography?

No, it is definitely a work of fiction. I would call it a fictionalized autobiography. It's hard to express this in a number, but considering the story as a whole, I would say, it's between 10 and 20 percent fictional. The detailed scenes of people interacting with each other are obviously mostly fictional, but their essence is always autobiographical. My goal was to give a truthful account of those years of my life so that they would paint a faithful portrait of me, and so I took liberties with the inessential aspects of the story while adhering strictly to the essential ones. I will add though that all the scenes of death and atrocities in the book are true, except in some cases I changed their chronology and a couple of times the personages. This was to build a more effective plot, aimed at creating a greater impact on the reader.

I will add once again, but without the details, so as not to give away the story for those who haven't read the book, that the final scene was literally a mere couple of minutes away from happening. Just a little longer, and I wouldn't be here, doing this interview with you. The horror of having been so close to that calamity has stayed with me for the rest of my life and was the chief impulse for my wanting to write the book and ultimately for doing it. It has changed me forever. Chills still run up my spine as I think of it.

How important is the novel for you?

As far as literary accomplishment is concerned, I feel that my two most important works of fiction are the 1993 novel *Three Blondes and Death* and the 2013 collection of fifteen interrelated mininovels *The Placebo Effect Trilogy*. They are the most original and most radical books of all I wrote. But for me personally, as far as emotional satisfaction is concerned, *Warm Arctic Nights* is the most important. As I explained earlier, I conceived it many years ago and felt I had to write it to explain not only to the world but also to myself who I was and where I came from. I felt deficient and extremely frustrated when I was unable to write it, and when I finally did, this huge bolder of shame and guilt I'd been carrying along for years rolled off my soul and I felt an enormous relief and liberation. I had finally done it and I was free of any debts or obligations! It was as if I was starting a new life as a writer.

But *Warm Arctic Nights* is also important to me as a historical document—as far as I know, it is the only work of fiction about pre-WWII Poland and WWII Ukraine, including flight to the West, told by someone who has lived through these events, and it is told as a purely personal story, without any political coloration. I think it

Yuriy Tarnawsky

should be of interest to Ukrainians and non-Ukrainians alike. It has been translated into Ukrainian by Maxym Nestelieiev for the Kyiv publishing house Tempora and is scheduled to be released this fall. It has also been translated into German.

What is the most interesting thing you have learned about yourself while writing this book?

What I learned from writing the book was that the most important person in my life, who shaped me the most, was my father and I dedicated the book to him. I had always known he played an important role in my life but didn't know how important it was. As I was writing the book, I realized that he was the person I admired above all other from my earliest childhood. I had always wanted to be like him and as I was growing up, I modeled myself on him. He is the prototype of what I am today. To summarize what that is—a man, physically and mentally tough, ruthlessly strict with himself, unwavering in adherence to his principles, and conscious of his duties as a male. There is a scene with a family of acrobats performing a difficult stunt in the first part of the book, the central figure in which is the husband/father, who carries the greatest burden. This is what I have in mind.

The dedication reads, "To the memory of my father who loved me more than anyone else." It is deliberately ambiguous and I feel that in this I may be right.

Has anyone or any work of art influenced you in writing this book?

Not directly. The book (its form) came out of my own writing, out of what I have learned over the years from the great writers of yesterday and my own hard work. As I said earlier, it finally moved when I decided to use the interview, or question and answer form. I had used this approach in my long 1975 poem *The Plumed Heart* and somehow felt it would work well here, which I feel it did. It enabled me to use the "if it doesn't please you, don't write it" criterion I employ in the genre of the mininovel which I developed. So, the book is a natural outcome of my own work. But in becoming the writer I am, I was certainly influenced by the works of others in all forms of art, in particular in literature and film. I learned reading by myself at the age of four, both in Polish and Ukrainian, and starting from then on read voraciously everything I could lay my hands on. First it was fables, but later adventure stories, historical works, especially those about Cossacks, and books on travel. I talk about it in the novel. The better-known international titles that come to mind are *Robinson Crusoe* (and its Ukrainian variant *Son of Ukraine*), *Children of Captain Grant*, *Jungle Books* (known in Ukrainian as *Brothers of Mowgli*) *Gulliver's Travels*, The *Adventures of Tom Sawyer* and *Huckleberry Finn,* a condensed version of *The Odyssey*, *Travels Through Central Asia* by Sven Hedin.... At the age of fourteen I read a book by Dostoyevsky *(The Devils)* and was so smitten by it that I read all of his books after that and stayed under his spell well into my twenties. I claim him to be my first literary progenitor. Then came Sartre and Kierkegaard and infatuation with Existentialism; Kafka; Proust's enormous opus; Kleist's meticulously structured prose; rediscovery of Hohol, in particular *Dead Souls*, traces of whose grotesqueness I find in my own work (I use the famous opening sentence of its second volume as an epigraph in my *Three Blondes and Death*); and Latin American fiction—Carpentier, Rulfo, Borges, García Márquez, Asturias.... I didn't like poetry until I came to this country and discovered it could be written in normal language without the potty-straining of meter and rhyme. Here Latin American poetry was the big discovery, in particular Neruda, my second progenitor, whose work was the impetus for my first, 1956, book *Life in the City*. Later came the discovery of Rimbaud, my third progenitor, and Surrealism. The influence of Surrealism came primarily through visual art (Dalí, de Chirico, Miró) and film (Buñuel, Cocteau). But film in general has had a strong influence on me (my tendency to be visual in my writing)—Bergman, Bresson, Satyajit Ray, Clair, Antonioni, Dovzhenko. And finally comes my fourth and most important progenitor—Johann Sebastian Bach, who deserves the full naming, the master of structure and emotions melded into an inseparable whole. I can only try to be an asymptote to him, forever striving to merge at infinity with his perfection.

So, as you see, I had a lot of help in writing *Warm Arctic Nights*. White Plains, NY

April 14, 2019

First published in Bulletin of the Shevchenko Scientific Society, *No. 46 (62), 2018. [The issue came out late.] Edited by Yuriy Tarnawsky.*

Anna Procyk is a Ukrainian-American historian.

INTERVIEW WITH MAXYM NESTELIEIEV

MN: You published this year two English-language novels, The Iguanas of Heat, *about Mexico and America, and* Warm Arctic Nights, *about Ukraine. These are very different texts that seem to have nothing in common except the language they're written in. What is for you the choosing of language and why didn't you write* Warm Arctic Nights *in Ukrainian?*

YT: When Ukraine became independent, I planned to fully integrate myself into Ukrainian literary life—bought myself an apartment in Kyiv and wanted to spend good part of the year there, but it didn't work out that way. Ukrainian literary establishment didn't want to accept me as one of its own. As they say in English, it gave me the cold shoulder. I remember, Ihor Rymaruk and I were having a chat in his office, there was a pause, and suddenly he said, totally unrelated to what we were speaking about earlier, "You're American." I was stunned. I had lived outside of Ukraine practically all my life, but had always called myself Ukrainian, wrote in Ukrainian, didn't belong to the Communist Party of the USSR and had never waved my party ticket, yelling at the top of my voice, "I'm for!" and suddenly I'm American? This really opened my eyes. But the main reason was that my books weren't being published. Aside from a book of selected poems published during the Communist years, I had a book of stories published thanks to my friend Volodymyr Tsybulko. All other, I had to pay for myself or they were published with Diaspora money. And even now I have been trying to find a publisher to republish the two volumes of my collected poetry in Ukrainian, but have had no offers. It's for the first time that Tempora is publishing one of my books, thanks to your efforts, for which I am most grateful.

But I must confess that it's easier for me now to write, in English. It's the language of the society I live in, and I consider my current writing as part of American literature, part of the literature of the Western world. In my English-language works, I'm American writer and writer of the Western world of Ukrainian origin. English language is a universal language and through it I can connect with practically all people. This is an important factor for me.

But I can't stop myself from commenting here on your contention that my two latest novels have nothing in common, namely, that they both end in a similar way—they're not fully resolved. And one more thing—each of their parts consists of fifteen chapters.

Warm Arctic Nights *has the form of an interview. Why is that form important to you?*

I first thought of the novel more than thirty years ago as a fictional version of the first ten years of my live, and although I tried to write it a number of times, I just couldn't make any headway because the autobiographical data was getting in the way of my

Yuriy Tarnawsky

imagination. Aside of the novel *Meningitis*, part of which has autobiographical data, none of my other books of fiction is based on my life. This fully unties my hands, and I can do what I want to delight the reader. The fact that I couldn't handle this subject really bothered me and made me feel inadequate. What kind of a writer am I, I though, if I can't write about my childhood?

Then, in the fall of 2017, I decided to give myself one more chance and intuitively thought of doing the book as an interview with myself. This way I was able to exclude subjects which were inessential and stick to only hose I thought important, and this opened up the floodgates of my imagination. The text flowed like a huge river and I finished the book in six months. I worked on the book after that, but the first draft was ready in February 2018.

During all those dozens of years I've been writing, I have learned to stick to the principle, "write down only what gives you pleasure and leave out everything else. This way you will at least please yourself." This approach has led me to discover the genre of the mininovel, in which I rely on short segments of text, augmented by *negative text,* that is, leaving out of important information which the reader has to supply himself. The question/answer form is a variant of that approach. Without it, I wouldn't have been able to write the novel.

A number of your books have been published by Journal of Experimental Fiction Books. How do you characterize your writing? Can it be called Postmodernist?

In my essay "Modernism is also a Humanism," I advance the thesis that there are two types of literary Postmodernism—artistic, that is, works that have artistic value, and commercial, or works of little, if any, such value, which are written for purely commercial reasons, such as those of Umberto Eco. According to this thesis, Postmodernism is the last phase of Modernism, which includes many characteristics of classical Modernism of the 1920-30's, in addition to new elements. I feel that my writing naturally grows out of classical Modernism—strict adherence to the free-verse form and Existentialism in poetry (the volume *Life in the City)* and plot-based Existentialism in fiction (the novel *Roads)*— to Postmodernism—language experiments and irrationality in poetry (the volume *Without Spain)* as well as language experiments in fiction (the novels *Meningitis,* which is built up of short stories, and *Three Blondes and Death*, based on numerology, both written in an artificial language). My most obviously Postmodernist works are the Ukrainian-language plays that make up the hexalogy *6x0,* which are patterned on Classical Greek drama. One of them, *Not Medea,* I translated into English and it was published and staged at the famous New York Mabou Mineas theater. The genre of the mininovel, which I mentioned earlier, in which *The Placebo-Effect Trilogy* is written, is almost emblematically Postmodernist—a

Yuriy Tarnawsky

structure based on associations, gaps in narration, style of narration that combines prose, dramatic dialogue, and poetry, and constant play with the reader with all sorts of allusions. The volume of poetry *Modus Tollens*, with the subtitle *Improvised Poetic Devices,* in which I force the reader to become an active co-author, is also an emblematically Postmodernist work. So, I think that I'm a Modernist, who grew into a Postmodernist.

You are known for your critical attitude toward the translation method of Mykola Lukash. You yourself have translated both poetry and prose. Should one approach the two genres differently?

People didn't understand me. I didn't criticize Lukash for his translations but because he insisted that that was the right way to translate Lorca into Ukrainian, that his adaptations in the style of 19th century Ukrainian poetry were the most adequate for Ukrainian readers. By this he negated or hid Lorca's Modernism, and even worse, denied the possibility of Modernism in Ukrainian poetry.

Poetry, especially traditional rhymed and metered poetry, is a unique confluence of phonetics and semantics in the language of the original. Ideally, you should something exactly like that in the translation, but this is practically impossible. Therefore, translating such poems, you have to make compromises in one or the other field, and asking which of them is more important generally is inappropriate. It depends on the particular case—which plays a more vital role there. The aim is to make a good translation. This task is precisely the work of the translator and how close the translation is to the original makes us able to decide how good it is—the closer, the better. (Adaptations sometimes may be a good solution, which is what Lukash actually did, but he didn't admit to it.) To translate free verse is much easier, because it isn't as restrictive phonetically.

Theoretically, it is much easier to translate prose, but not all prose translations are good. The translator has to catch the rhythm of the narration (its syntactic and lexical structure) and render it adequately. This isn't a simple matter, and I'm inclined to say that both genres are difficult to translate.

Which books do you like to reread? Which of the contemporary American writers deserve being read or translated into Ukrainian? Which contemporary Ukrainian writers would you recommend to be read to strangers?

Unfortunately, I read very little these days--lack of time and conscious abstaining, because reading interferes with your own writing. But in the past, I used to reread most frequently Rimbaud, his *Illuminations*, which I used to carry with me on my business travels like the Bible. I also used to read Flaubert, Stendhal, Hohol

Yuriy Tarnawsky

(his *Dead Souls)*, Kleist, Proust, Joyce, Beckett, Neruda, Lorca, Borges, Asturias, Carpentier. As to contemporary writers, I would advise reading my colleagues from the early Fiction Collective— Baumbach, Sukenik, Katz (his marvelous autobiographical book *Memoirrhoids)*, Aias-Misson (a likewise wonderful autobiographical book *Autobiography of a Charact from Fiction,* for which I wrote the afterword*)*, plus the novels of Eckhard Gerdes (one of them includes "Shevchenko's Death Mask"), Markson *(Wittgenstein's Mistress)*.

As to contemporary Ukrainian authors—I would probably suggest the most popular names, because I've read too little of contemporary Ukrainian literature to be more specific.

You've been active in all literary genres, but do you have a favorite one? Do you accept the thesis about the death of the novel? Which for you is the great American novel and do you think there exists the great Ukrainian novel?

My favorite genre is fiction, but, as I said, I incorporate in my fiction works elements of both drama and poetry, and devote in them as much attention to language as in poems. And in general, in my fiction works I revert to poetic devices whenever necessary, since they are so effective, and I think that's the way it should be. Just look at Homer's *Iliad* and *Odyssey*. They are just magnificent works of art. It doesn't matter whether they are poetry or prose.

The distinction between poetry and prose is artificial and relatively new. What is natural, is a work of literature, which can be long or short, that's all, and working on it the author is free to use any means at his disposal.

The time of "great novels" was the nineteenth century, especially in English, French, and Russian literatures. Trying to import this notion into later, younger literatures is pointless. There may be some justification to claim that *Moby Dick* is the great American novel, but even among its contemporaries there are none that come close to it, whereas in the three literatures I mentioned, there are many that may have a claim.

For me the best Ukrainian novel of the nineteenth century is *Lyuboratski,* but I wouldn't call it the great Ukrainian novel.

Is the novel dead? If you consider the nineteenth century novel as the novel, then I think, yes, it is dead, and so much the better. May it rest in peace.

Warm Arctic Nights is a memoir of your childhood. Do you plan to write one about your adolescence and adulthood or about the New York Group?

All of my prose books are about myself, except it's all camouflaged under fiction. I like it this way. I will mention, however, that I have

Yuriy Tarnawsky

dealt with my adolescence in the same way as in this book in my first, Ukrainian-language novel *Roads*. In some sense, it picks up where *Warm Arctic Nights* leaves off. The boy has somehow managed to survive, became German, and struggled between being a bourgeois and an Existentialist. After that, the chronology is pretty mixed up. But I never had a need to write about the New York Group and I doubt that I ever will.

What advice would you give to young, aspiring authors? What is a must reading for someone who wants to become a writer?

For God's sake, my dear young friend, if there is any chance that you don't have to be a writer, stay away from this métier as far as possible. It will bring you no good. You'll crave recognition and financial gain, but if your writing will have artistic value, you almost certainly will not get them. You will bring out of your life only bitterness toward yourself and the world. Choose a profession which benefits you and the society, start a family, have children, and appreciate the world for how beautiful it is.

But if not, if you absolutely have to write and are condemned to walk this thorny path, write so that it'll bring you joy. Rely on your own judgement and taste. Listen to yourself and not to others. Write for yourself and enjoy what you have written, and if you're lucky, you may experience moments of enlightenment, such as others can't even dream about.

Read the great masters of the past, the Greek Classics, Shakespeare, the great English, French, and Russian novelists, others, the modern Classics, but stay away from your contemporaries, especially those of your age. You'll wind up chasing their tails.

First published in Ukrainian in LitAkcent, *September 17, 2019. Translated and edited by Yuriy Tarnawsky.*

Maxym Nestelieiev is a Ukrainian translator and literary scholar, specializing in American Postmodernism, author of the Ukrainian-language translation of Warm Arctic Nights.

INTERVIEW WITH BOHDANA ROMANTSOVA

BR: During this year's publishers' bookfair we presented a Ukrainian-language translation of your novel Warm Artic Nights, *in which you tell the story of your childhood in Pre-WWII Poland and the war years in Ukraine. After the idyllic account of the early years, you describe the gruesome events of pogroms and executions that came later. What did writing this novel mean to you? Do you feel that a writer has an obligation to become a witness of historical events, play the role of Fortinbras?*

YT: I got the idea of writing *Warm Arctic Nights* more than thirty years ago. One day I heard an ad on the radio promoting Caribbean cruises in which the phrase "you'll be able to enjoy the cool tropical nights." This struck me as a blatant oxymoron, and the phrase "warm arctic nights" immediately popped up in my mind, which evoked memories from my childhood. I decided to write about them, if not perhaps right away, but soon afterwards. So, I sat down at the table (at that time I wrote things out by hand) and started writing. But I just couldn't make any headway. The facts from my life were so powerful that I couldn't convert them into fiction, and was just noting them down unaltered.

The topic was so deeply embedded inside me, however, that I couldn't set myself free from it. I set it aside for a while, tried it another three or four times, and finally began to fear that I wouldn't be able to do it. This really bothered me, and I thought, what kind of a writer are you if you can't write about something what you really want? In September 2017, I looked at my watch and told myself, time's passing, Yuriy, you'll either write this book now, or never.

I closed my eyes and asked myself, what do I want to talk about?—About the room, where I was born, which I barely remembered. I asked myself then what did that room look like, and promptly answered my question. Then I realized that I couldn't continue my story as in traditional novels, but had to proceed with posing myself little questions, like the first one, and answering them, almost as during a session with a psychoanalyst. I finished the first draft in six months, and hardly changed it at all after that. The book was a huge catharsis for me, because the first ten years of my life are its foundation. I experienced in them the most beautiful and the most horrific events I have lived through.

What was the reaction to the book in the US?

It came out this May, so I didn't have time to promote it. I worked first with Maxym on the Ukrainian translation [Maxym Nestelieiev translated the book into Ukrainian for the publishing house Tempora] and then with Christian Weise on the German version. I know that a big review is forthcoming in *American Book*

Yuriy Tarnawsky

Review, and then the book is supposed be reviewed in the on-line zine *The Collagist.*

In the US, unless the author vigorously promotes his book, it is bound to be forgotten. When a book doesn't sell during the first three months, it is usually sold for pulp. My situation is somewhat different. I've been published by independent noncommercial houses and, for instance, my novel *Meningitis*, which came out in 1978 is still available.

In Warm Arctic Nights *there is a lot about Ukraine of the 1940's. How is Ukraine represented in contemporary American literature, assuming if it's represented at all?*

It is not. It's true that Askold Melnyczuk's novel *What Is Told*, which came out a few years ago, paints a somewhat different picture Ukraine than mine, although even in it there isn't that much about it. Right now, people know about Ukraine through Maidan, but in fiction, I don't know of anyone writing about it.

When you wrote Warm Arctic Nights, *was it your aim to bring Ukraine into reality the American culture?*

Yes, I wanted the world to know how it was. Ukrainians are often labeled as antisemites, accused of taking part in the execution of Jews as well as other war crimes. I never witnessed anything like that. It's true that the local police carried out the orders of the Germans, such as herding Jews. But they also rounded up Ukrainians to be sent to Germany for forced labor. On the other hand, Jewish ghettos likewise had Jewish police, which carried out German orders. But I never saw any special antisemitism among Ukrainians. I think, however, that Russian antisemitism is an institutional phenomenon. There were undoubtedly instances of individual antisemitism among Ukrainians, but it wasn't systemic. And I wanted to describe this.

You sometimes mention in your interviews that you often meet with Ukrainian diaspora public in New York. What is its status nowadays? Is it capable of exerting influence on the US government's policies and lobby Ukrainian interests?

I started writing in English soon after I came to the US, when I was eighteen years old. But I didn't know how to get published, so I kept it for myself. But then I came across Ukrainian magazines, such as *National Tribune*, the forerunner of *Suchasnist,* which was edited by Ivan Koshelivets, and I began writing in Ukrainian and sent it in there. It was published and this put a brake on my English-language writing. Eventually my colleagues and I founded the New York Group and I devoted myself exclusively to Ukrainian literature. In the 1970's, when I published my first novel *Roads*, the Diaspora cultural life began to subside. The young ones turned to English, the old ones stopped writing or passed away, and right now there are no Ukrainian cultural movements in America. Members of the fourth wave of immigrants aren't involved in literature. Diaspora's activities are largely exclusively political—it exerts pressure on members of the Congress and, to a lesser degree, on the President. I think that Ukrainian Diaspora had important influence on the re-emergence of Ukraine and on outside the support, it was and is getting.

Is there a difference between the older generation of Diaspora Ukrainians, those, who immigrated in the 1950's and 1960's, and the recent, economically motivated immigrants?

The difference is enormous. These are two totally different kinds of people. The new immigrants have left home for personal, economic reasons, whereas the previous wave was politically motivated, it was the Ukrainian elite, which wanted to preserve itself, so as to serve Ukraine. It included such people as Yuriy Lavrinenko, Yuriy Shevelov, Ulas Samchuk, Yuriy Kosach, and many others. The cultural life in the Diaspra, in particular literary, was very vibrant. Eventually there appeared such important institutions as the Harvard Ukrainian Research Institute and the Canadian Institute of Ukrainian Studies, which play an important role in Ukrainian scholarly and political life to this day.

I would like to dwell some more on the subject of Ukrainian cultural life in the US, talking about the New York Group. In the textbooks of Ukrainian literature there is little space devoted to these authors, and at universities the Group is studied more as a literary phenomenon, rather than a link that joins the generations of the sixties and eighties with the millennials and the contemporaries. Why is that? Is it because of the complexity and hermeticism of the New Yorkers? The distancing of themes? If so, then where does this distancing come from?

You are right to say that the New York Group, which was founded by Bohdan Boychuk and me, hasn't had as much influence on Ukrainian literature as it deserves. The name, by the way, was my idea. I wanted to stress the break with tradition through the geographical break. I was younger than Boychuk and more radical, and just couldn't write traditional rhymed poetry and from the very beginning wrote in free verse. In the West, Modernism was such a powerful movement that we couldn't help being influenced by it. As a result, there arose this fairly radical school in Ukrainian poetry, influenced by Latin American, French, and American literatures.

When Ukraine gained its independence, I was sure that Modernism will come out the winner and was surprised that everyone was still talking of Lina Kostenko as the paragon of greatness. I have nothing against Ms. Kostenko, but the young generation stil thought that this was the kind of poetry they should be writing. I never suspected that such a thing would happen. I think that the Group was too radical to be accepted at that stage by Ukrainians. The second reason appears to be the fact that we come from America, from the West, and are considered strangers. I was personally told once that I was American. I was having a conversation with Ihor Rymaruk, there was a pause, and suddenly he said, "You're an American." I was shocked. Why am I an American? I have always considered myself Ukrainian, I write in Ukrainian, I didn't wave my Communist party ticket, yelling "I'm for!" This really hurt me, because I realized what was going on. This is a telling example. Later people began showing some interest in us, but these were mostly members of the young generation. The literary establishment never did warm up to us. I think that competition and jealousy were the factors that played a role in all of this.

You are stating very firmly that you are Ukrainian. But shouldn't we speak of a complex heterogenic identity when we talk about your writing? Did I understand you correctly?

I'm 100% Ukrainian, but I am also American. This isn't a contradiction. I am American citizen and feel fully obligated to what that entails. This country accepted me and gave me everything I have. It never mistreated me and didn't repress me for being Ukrainian. I am very grateful to it for that. I consist of three parts. The first is the me from my Ukrainian childhood, as described in *Warm Arctic Nights*, and my writing from the New

York Group years. The second is American, an IBM employee and University professor. And the third--me as part of American literature, which I consider as part of the literature of the West. English is the *lingua franca* of our times. In it I write for all people of the Western world. Ukraine is also part of that world, so that I continue being a Ukrainian writer. I come to Ukraine through English, and now through Maxym's translation of *Warm Arctic Nights.*

Serhiy Zadan, recalling how he came upon your book U ra na *at the beginning of the 1990's, said that he found the patriotism in it totally different from that of the Sixtiers. And this is exactly what Ukrainian literature needed. So, what is your take on patriotism in poetry?*

One of the reasons for how I feel about Ukrainian literature is the standardized patriotism you find in it. I was supposed to speak in the poem about certain topics and treat them in a certain way, but I wanted to write about what I felt. When the Chornobyl accident happened, I was shaken to the core—I realized for the first time that Ukraine was in the danger of disappearing from the face of the earth any minute, if it hadn't done so already. It was my personal emotions that were the reason why I was writingt he book. *U ra na* is *Ukraina,* from which two letters have disappeared, as in the neon sign of a semi abandoned hotel, which is about to be shut down. The poem, which came out in the Kharkiv publishing house Berezil was disliked by both Ukrainian "patriots" and ukrainephobes. Almost all of the run was immediately bought out and destroyed—I don't know if by the former or the latter. *U ra na* is full of anger. I speak in it about Ukraine both with love and with hatred. My patriotism is a patriotism of personal feelings.

You consider yourself to be an author of alternative literature. What are the characteristics of such writing?

First of all, disobedience of conventional rules. You do what you consider necessary, and not what someone tells you. For me to write something is like proving a theorem. In mathematics you try to do it as elegantly as possible. I try to do this in my writing. This is the only rule I follow.

Are you one of those authors, who demand of your readers utmost intellectual involvement?

Absolutely. I write for the select few. An important factor in my writing is that the readers must be able to recreate the work in their minds. I supply all the elements and instructions, and they do the rest. This is especially true of short fictions, which I call *mininovels*. They are based on *negative* text, that is, text that hasn't been written down. I construct short chapters, say, ten to fifteen of them, which are complete in themselves, but are not explicitly connected with each other. For instance, a character may be alive in one chapter and is dead in another. So, the reader has to imagine on his own how this happened. But this requires of him to cooperate with me by relying on his imagination. So, I take constant risks.

You often revert to the subject of memory and reappraisal of experience. To what degree do Warm Arctic Nights *belong to the practice of writing about memory in contemporary American literature?*

My two favorite books of contemporary American writers deal with memory. My close friend Steve Katz—unfortunately he died in August this year—has a wonderful book, called *Memoirrhoids* The book consists of short concentrated fragments, not arranged in chronological order. There's in it even a little about me. The second book is also by a good friend of mine Alain Arias-Misson, a Belgian-American author who used to live in America, but now resides in France, and writes in English. He has a magnificent work, called *Autobiography of a Character from Fiction*, which unites tendencies of *In Search of Lost Time, Alice in Wonderland* and many other works. I wrote an Afterword to it. My book is different, but these two books, in some sense, gave me an impetus to write mine.

The American university professor and author Steve Tomasula said that you, like a cat, have lived nine lives. You write fiction, non-fiction, poetry, plays, do translations. Which of these genres

Yuriy Tarnawsky

is the most important to you? Is such a broad field of interest intended and fundamental?

Yes, it is intended. I am interested in all these genres, but like writing fiction the most. Poetry, it's relaxing, giving out a scream, and smiling. But fiction—it's a chance to create worlds that will go on being. I've lived more than nine lives, because every work of fiction I have written is a life which I have created myself.

First published in Ukrainian in Ukrajins'kyj tyzhden'*, 40 (620) 4-10.10 2019. Translated and edited by Yuriy Tarnawsky.*

Bohdana Romantsova is an editor at Tempora, the publisher of the Ukrainian-language translation of Warm Arctic Nights.

CHYTOMO INTERVIEW WITH OLEKSANDR MYMRUK

Yuriy Tarnawsky, the renowned Ukrainian-American writer, one of the founders of the New York Group, is visiting this year's 26th Lviv Book Forum to present the Ukrainian-language translation of his novel Warm Arctic Nights. *The original English-language version of the book came out in February of this year, and today, thanks to Tempora Publishing and the translator Maxym Nestelieiev, the text is available to Ukrainian readers. Yuriy Tarnawsky is not a frequent visitor to Ukraine, so* Chytomo *couldn't pass up the opportunity to chat with him about his new book, his literary plans, and literature in general.*

OM: Warm Arctic Nights *is an autobiographical novel, and one has to say that for admirers of your writing somewhat of a surprise. It's true that in your earlier works, such as* Meningitis *and* Roads, *you can find autobiographical elements, but for us here, your name is associated with more hermetic and experimental work. How did it happen that you felt compelled to write in this genre?*

YT: I got the idea for the novel some thirty years ago and tried to write it many times, but wasn't able to make any headway precisely because of the autobiographical data. It stood in my way and wouldn't let my imagination work freely. This bothered me a lot, because I felt a great need to put down on paper an account of the first ten and a half years of my life, especially because of

49

the traumatic nature of the last four of them. I tried to write the book in the standard narrative style, but it would come out very awkward and stiff. Then in the fall of 2017 I told myself that I'm giving myself one last chance to deal with the topic, and in despair started putting down on paper only what came to my mind. I would pose myself a question about something I remembered, and answer it, and the text suddenly began to move like ice on a frozen river in springtime. And so, it flowed to the end in this question-and-answer interview form and I finished the book in six months.

Tell us some more about the question/answer style that forms the basis of the novel. It reminded me of your poetry cycled Questionnaires *which as structured in a similar way, like filling in blanks in a medical questionnaire.* Warm Arctic Nights *isn't quite the same, but there is some similarity.*

In my appearances here, I mentioned time and again that I couldn't write the novel because of the straightjacket of autobiographical facts. My imagination just couldn't work feely. Only when I asked myself the question, How was the room? and answered it, which became the beginning of the text, was I able to write on, because then the memories and associations took over the control over the writing.

You're right in saying that *Questionnaires* are in some way similar to this style of writing. Here again associations take over the process. And I also have another work written the same way—the long poem *Plumed Heart.* I didn't base myself consciously on these works, but they obviously had some influence on the novel

At your appearances you frequently said that the novel is very cinematographic and that the episodes you describe are treated visually. How much were you influenced by visual art (painting, film, and so on)?

Originally, I wanted to make films, but physical difficulties connected with this made it impossible, and I began to treat writing as descriptions of films, which I wanted to make. In general, I perceive the world visually and render it as such. Painting and film had just as important an influence on me as literature.

During the presentation in Kyiv you asked me if the scene with a little boy being bathed in Fellini's *8½* influenced a similar one I have in the novel. I smiled then in response, because I realized that it definitely did. In the novel the episode has a fully autobiographical origin, but I love the scene in Fellini's movie and I'm sure it influenced what I wrote—suggested the bathing I describe. But it was on a completely subconscious level.

You have a strong technical background—you worked for many years at IBM. Has that experience manifested itself in your

writing? Does technical background help writing, or does it hinder it?

I think that my technical background has a fundamental influence on my writing. Many critics stress the structural clarity of my work, it's "engineering" nature, which is clearly connected with my profession.

My technical schooling and work taught me to pay attention to form and I carried this over into literature. This is important to me and I think it makes my writing more interesting, makes it stand out.

It's interesting that the presentation of your novel at the Forum was placed in the non-fiction category, although the book obviously is not devoid of fiction. What is more prevalent in it— facts from your life, or imagination?

I didn't know that. It's completely wrong. I called the book a novel, and it is a literary work of a genre, called in English "fictionalized autobiography." It's perhaps 80-90% autobiographical, but I made crucial changes in the chronology and characters, and all the details are of course completely dreamed up, although they are 100% true in their essence. So, when I say that 80-90% of the book are facts from my life, I mean sticking to the essence of my biography. But all deaths and atrocities I describe are exactly as they happened.

I made these changes in order to make the narration more effective, have a greater impact on the reader. This kind of thing is what makes fiction different from a memoir. Something dreamt up may be more truthful than reality. That's why I wrote the book this way.

Lately there has been a trend in Ukrainian literature to write about "family memory" and childhood. Many poets and fiction writers write about their early, naïve endeavors, share their memories about long-gone relatives, grandmothers and grandfathers. Among these there are books we are used to call "family sagas." Why has this topic become so popular?

I don't know, and I didn't know this is happening in Ukraine. In my case, this was a purely personal decision and need. It looks like the same is happening to other people and they feel a need to express themselves this way.

At the presentations in Lviv and Kyiv you said that the historical period described in the novel isn't much covered in Ukrainian literature. Do you think that elucidating this period will lead to a revaluation of our history, make us see it from another angle?

Yuriy Tarnawsky

It's hard to predict the future, at least it is for me, but judging by how Ukrainian society is behaving right now, I doubt that my novel will have any effect on it, and I mean this not only in historical sense, but also cultural. The literary aspects of the book will attract the interest of only those who like something new in literature, and the establishment and general society won't pay any attention to it. And as to the historical—I'm sure, the book will disappear like a stone tossed into water.

I know that in the past you used to translate yourself (did Ukrainian-language versions of your English-language works), but Warm Arctic Nights *was translated by Maxym Nestelieiev. Why he? How strongly did you control the translation. Was it possible to render in the translation the richness of the original?*

I have too little time to translate myself, and I started to hate the task. I feel it's a waste of time to grind over something that's already been ground, and I am very grateful to Maxym for having taken on this task. I read what he did very carefully, and we considered jointly any problems that arose, so that the translation came out very exact and close to the original. We have called it "authorized translation."

Have you noticed that in the past few years the contribution of the New York Group and of you personally has been reexamined and has received a new valuation? Some documentary films have

been made, new books about the group and by its members have
come out, you're being discussed at literary presentation, and
Emma Anmdiyevska has even received the Shevchenko prize.
Can we say "the great homecoming of the New Hork Group" has
finally happened?

Well, perhaps there has been an improvement, thanks to the
younger generation, such as Oleksandr Fraze-Frazenko, Ihor
Kotyk, Tanya Ostapchuk, and a few others. But the literary
establishment still doesn't notice and accept us and we remain on
the margins of literary life in Ukraine. Andiyevska, comically,
maintains that she's not a member of the group, so maybe that's
why she got the prize.

In the past you said that you haven't been paying much attention
to what is taking place in Ukrainian literature right now. Has
anything changed? Are there some Ukrainian texts and authors
you have read?

No, I really have not read anything new in Ukrainian literature
recently. I simply don't have time. I also don't read much of
anything else either, except the work of some of my close
American friends, out of friendship and interest.

What advice would you give to emerging Ukrainian writers?

Yuriy Tarnawsky

I would urge them not to imitate the writing of others because it became popular, but to create something organic and their own. And also, not to write for the sake of gain, but for that of literature, to write, obeying the rules of literature, the way a mathematician proves a theorem, not trying to please others, but doing it, while obeying the rules of mathematics, as simply and elegantly as possible. A well-written literary work is an elegantly proven theorem.

What are you working on right now?

I am working on a poetry collection in English called *Modus Quasi Ponens*, which is a response and antithesis to the collection of heuristic poetry *Modus Tollens* that came out in 2013. Here, in contrast to poems written in short lines, which writhe on the page like chopped up rainworms, you have blocks of calm narrative prose. Peace sometimes comes along with age.

First published in Ukrainian in Chytomo, *October 1t6, 2019. Translated and edited by Yuriy Tarnawsky. Oleksandr Mymruk is a Ukrainian writer and editor.*

SHEVCHENKO SCIENTIFIC SOCIETY MEMBER OF THE MONTH INTERVIEW

Hometown: White Plains, NY

Current Position: Retiree, IBM Corporation, Columbia University

Professional Interests: Transformational-Generative Grammar, Natural Language Processing, Literary Theory, Innovative Writing

Why did you decide to join the Shevchenko Scientific Society?

Having been active in the Ukrainian Diaspora community in general and as a writer in particular, once I became a scientist, first as electrical engineer and then computer scientist and linguist, it was natural for me to feel I should join the society. It was a decision based both on patriotic and scientific grounds. The benefits, so to speak, were both professional and social. I was able to promote my literary and scientific works (doing literary readings and having my PhD dissertation and books of literary essays published) and meet with member colleagues at after-event receptions.

What do you value about membership in the Society? What is your most memorable Society's event or publication?

Yuriy Tarnawsky

In my opinion, the Society's most important achievement is fomenting scholarly and scientific work in Ukraine by funding student scholarships, individual research, and scholarly and scientific publications. I have particularly enjoyed the yearly symposiums commemorating Taras Shevchenko. Another series I enjoyed a lot were the five presentations by Dr. Volodymyr Mezentsev on the Baturyn archeological excavations sponsored by the society.

The Society has published many valuable works but perhaps the most important one is *Encyclopedia of Ukrainian Diaspora*.

How did your interest in Ukrainian culture and society influence your career path?

I started out as a Ukrainian-language writer, being influenced (drawn-in) by such publications as the literary supplement to the Munich *Suchasna Ukrajina* edited by Ivan Koshelivets, which later morphed into the important publications *Literaturna Hazeta* and *Suchasnist'*. Through Koshelivets, I became friends with Yuriy Lavrinenko, who made me aware of the outstanding cultural developments in the 1920-30's Ukraine which made a strong impression on me. Without this I would have been an English-language writer from the beginning.

Professionally, I have not been influenced by my Ukrainian background. I did my undergraduate studies in Electrical Engineering at Newark College of Engineering which ultimately grew into New Jersey Institute of Technology. I started working on transistor circuits at the IBM T. J. Watson Research Center in Poughkeepsie, NY, in 1956, but soon transferred to the newly-formed Russian-to-English Machine Translation project, where I managed groups of lexicographers and linguists at IBM, the USAF Language School in Syracuse, NY, and the Library of Congress. Ultimately, sponsored by IBM, I studied theoretical linguistics at New York University, obtaining a PhD degree in 1982, after defending my Transformational-Generative Grammar dissertation Knowledge Semantics. Afterwards, I continued working at IBM in the area of Artificial Intelligence, primarily on Natural-Language Processing.

What is your current research/work project?

I left IBM in 1992 under an early retirement program and from 1993-1996 taught Ukrainian literature and culture courses at Columbia University. As part of that work, I wrote a series of papers devoted to Ukrainian literature most of which were published in the book of essays *Kvity xoromu* (Piramida, 2012), which was sponsored by the Society. The English-language book of essays *Claim to Oblivion* (JEF Books, 2016) consists largely of articles dealing with theoretical issues of literature, in particular language use. *Literary Yoga* (JEF Books, 2018) is a manual of Creative Writing.

In 2016, NaUKMA published a Ukrainian-language translation of my dissertation under the title *Znannjeva semantyka*. The translation was done under my supervision, with a portion translated by me. In connection with this work, I developed an extensive English-Ukrainian and Ukrainian-English dictionary of Transformational-Generative Grammar terms, first such in Ukrainian, which was published in the book. The publication was sponsored by the Society. A recent, still unpublished article "Toward a Knowledge-Based Semantic Theory," subtitled "How We Understand Each Other" deals with the important subject of knowledge acquisition.

As to my literary activities, in 2019 I published two English-language novels with JEF Books, both of which had been many years in the making—*Warm Arctic Nights* and *The Iguanas of Heat*. The first is a fictionalized semiautobiographical account of my childhood and the second an ostensible suspense story which is actually a deconstructional study of a sterile marriage. *Warm Arctic Nights* was published the same year by Tempora in an authorized Ukrainian-language translation by Maxym Nestelieiev under the title *Tepli poljarni nochi*. A German-language version of the novel, *Warme Arktische Nächte*, translated by Christian Weise, on which I also collaborated, was published by Edition Noëma/*ibdem*-Verlag in 2020.

Currently I am working on an English-language novel *Sebastian in a Dream* inspired by Georg Trakl's poem *"Sebastian im Traum"* and patterned on J. S. Bach's *Goldberg Variations*.

What career advice would you give for new members of the Shevchenko Scientific Society?

I would strongly urge young scholars in/from Ukraine to stay as far away as possible from the Soviet traditions and think of themselves as part of the new, still future Ukraine and thus part of the Western World. This applies to the topics they devote themselves to as well as the way they handle them.

First published in Shevchenko Scientific Society Bulletin, January, 2021

INTERVIEW WITH LORENZO POMPEO

LP: Since your life is divided between two worlds, the Ukrainian one and the USA one, so different and so distant, how are these two worlds melted in your literary creation in prose and poetry?

YT: I have lived outside of Ukraine since the age of 10 and have learned to be a Ukrainian and a member of the surrounding culture at the same time. Somehow, it was never that difficult for me to do that. We settled in Germany upon fleeing Ukraine, and I attended German High School. I came to the US just after I turned 18, and right away went to college. I learned English quickly, and within a few years began writing in that language, without knowing how to get published. But there were opportunities for me to get published in Ukrainian, so I devoted more effort to writing in my native language. But eventually, the pull toward English got stronger, and I wrote in both languages, often translating my own works from one to the other, so that I became a bilingual, Ukrainian-English writer. In recent years, I have switched over almost exclusively to English, and concentrate primarily on prose—a path that most writers seem to follow as they grow older.

Which part of the Ukrainian literary tradition do you think is most linked with your literary creation? Which part of the American one?

It seems to me that Ukrainian literature has not had a significant influence on my writing. I found it to be too traditional and was attracted by the modernist currents in Western literature. In fact, I started to write in Ukrainian in order to change Ukrainian literature, to make it more like what attracted me in the other languages. In my early years, I was actually not affected very much by American literature, but by German, French, and Spanish, in particular Latin American poetry.

Do you think that poetry can be expressed only in the mother language or also in a language learned later?

I think you can do both, and even be better in the new language, if you master it well. But here "master" is a subjective term. You don't have to know the language like a native speaker, but master it in your own way, create a private language of your own and become a master of it.

Do you think that a poet is able to translate his own poems in a different language?

Oh yes, definitely. I have been doing it myself for years and much of my poetry is written in both languages. The two versions are usually very close, but sometimes there may be important subtle differences.

Yuriy Tarnawsky

Speaking about translation, do you think your poems are "translatable" and, through a good translation, also accessible to a non-Ukrainian and non-USA public?

My poetry is primarily image-based, with little reliance on phonetics, and so it's relatively easy to translate. In my poetry I also often tackle common contemporary themes, which make it easily accessible to readers of different cultures. I consider myself a writer of Western Culture, who writes in Ukrainian and English, so my writing should be accessible to people of the Western World.

Have you noticed any substantial differences when you are conceiving and writing a poem in English or Ukrainian?

No, I seem to be able to express myself equally effective in either language, although right now I feel myself more comfortable writing prose in English than in Ukrainian. Ukrainian language has undergone big changes in the last 50 years or so, and[GT1] since I live outside of Ukraine, my "private" Ukrainian is a bit too different. I think it's fine for poetry, where language can be very individual, but may seem too idiosyncratic in prose.

What is your current relationship with Ukrainian language?

I use it freely in everyday life, at home or with friends, but lately have been writing only in English, primarily prose, but also some poetry.

Do you think that for a poet who writes in Ukrainian the language is a problem linked exclusively to the sphere of artistic expression or also to the historical-political one?

I think that a poet should be concerned only with what he is trying to say.

Who is the poet to whom you think you were indebted when you started writing poetry?

I was influenced most strongly by Georg Trakl, Pablo Neruda, and then, and most profoundly, by Arthur Rimbaud.

Your poetry seems linked to a philosophical dimension. Were there any philosophers that have inspired you in your writing?

I was strongly influenced by Existentialism, in particular by Jean-Paul Sartre, his novels and philosophical writings, as summarized in the article "Existentialism is a Humanism."

Do you think that poetry can and should circulate in a wider circle of readers or that circulation in a niche of readers is inevitable?

Yuriy Tarnawsky

I think poetry should address itself to the needs of the poet. So, it should find its reader milieu naturally, by itself, be it wide or narrow.

Many critics have pointed out in your collection "Poems about Nothing" a tendency towards "pictorial" representation. Do you think that poetry should be connected to the figurative arts, and in particular to contemporary art?

It depends on the poet, whatever he wants to do, or does. I have always been visually oriented, and that's why visual elements are so strong in my writing. But I don't try to imitate art, unless I am writing a poem about a particular painting.

Among the avant-garde movements of the twentieth century, the one to which your poetry seems to be closest is Surrealism. Do you believe that your poetry is somehow connected or has any relationship with Surrealism?

Definitely so. I was extremely attracted to Surrealism, especially the art and cinema, and it has certainly colored my writing. One of the things that attracted me to Latin American poetry is its "non-rational" nature, which, although not officially Surrealist, to me has much in common with the latter. So, I would credit such poets as Neruda as having made me a Surrealist.

First published as "Yuriy Tarnawsky, poet in the balance," in Il Vascello Fantasma, *June, 2021.*

Lorenzo Pompeo is an Italian editor and translator.

INTERVIEW WITH LORENZO POMPEO ABOUT NERUDA

LP: In your poem "When the Poet Pablo Neruda Is no Longer with Us" you paid a tribute to the Chilean poet. Is your poetry somehow in debt to Pablo Neruda or any other Latin-American poet, such as Octavio Paz?

YT: Very much so. I came the US from Germany in 1952 at the age of 18, having been exposed exclusively to traditional rhymed poetry, to which I had an instinctive aversion, thinking it was silly to count syllables and find words that ended alike in order to express your pains and fears. It looked like a silly childish game to me, and I had no desire to play it. Delving into the wonderfully accessible public libraries in America, I quickly discovered that there was another way to write poetry—expressing it in the language you used in daily life, with your family, friends, and enemies, as well as in your mind, talking to yourself in grief, and anger, and joy. These were at first English-language poets, especially American, such as Whitman, Edgar Lee Masters, Sandburg, and e. e. cummings, and somewhat later Pound and Eliot, but almost parallel to it, international poets in translation, which, in the form customary in books in English, was always accompanied by the original text, which I found useful because I could reconstruct the original. Here, for some unknown reason, I was most attracted by Spanish language poetry, especially that of Latin America, of which there was more and which I found more appealing. Its language was closer to my way of thinking, dealt more with existential issues, and frequently reverted to figures of speech for which I appeared to have an inborn preference. The poets that I remember I was especially drawn to were Salvador Novo, Cesar Vallejo, Vicente Huidobro, and most ardently Pablo Neruda, whose work ultimately became the example, on which I began to model my own work. I got to know Octavio Paz somewhat later, when I had already developed my poetic language, and I don't think he impacted my writing to any degree.

How precisely did Neruda influence you?

Since my late teens I had been preoccupied with the notion of dying, and it got to be more bothersome as I entered into my late teens, when I came to America, and death was one of the major topics in Neruda's writing, so I couldn't get enough of reading his poems, dealing with this subject. I remember vividly such poems as *"Galope muerto"* with its opening lines *"Como cenizas, como mares poblándose,"* and *"Sólo la muerte,"* starting with *"Hay cementerios solos"* and ending with the magnificent *"en donde está esperando, vestida de admirante,"* where the missing subject *"la muerte"* is clearly spelled out in five lines earlier. (The quotation sounds better in English translation – "where death is waiting, dressed like an admiral.") There were other topics too, dear to my heart, related to existential issues, for instance. the poem "Waking around," with its title in English, as well as love, dealt with in an organic, earthy manner. These opened the floodgates of my imagination, and I couldn't stop myself from writing. In probably less than two years I had a book of poems ready, which I called *«Життя в місті»*, that is, "Life in the City," partially influenced by Neruda's *"Residencia en la tierra,"* but also by Sartre's existentialism ("life") and American urbanism ("city").

But there was also another feature in Neruda's poetry, which I found perhaps even more enticing—the way he saw the world and talked about it. He wasn't describing it in the normal fashion, where the words have their common meaning, but in clusters of them that like those shriveled up, scrawny-looking clumps of paper that turn into beautiful flowers when put in water, blossomed into fantastic evocative images. This is communicating in associations, and it reminded me of Ukrainian folklore, songs, spells, and incantations, which I loved since childhood—and also of French Surrealism with which I was beginning to get acquainted. This kind of seeing and speaking was natural to me and although I didn't practice it much in my first book, it became the dominate feature of my later writing, both in poetry and prose.

Who are your favorite Latin-American poets?

Neruda was and remains still my favorite, although my tastes have changed and I've become critical of some of his work infused with politics. I've been away from that world for a long time, but as recall, I liked Vicente Huidobro a lot, as well Cesar Vallejo, Jorge Carrera Andrade, Octavio Paz, Nicolás Guillen, as well as many others, who for me formed a school, so that I treated them almost as one. I loved the culture that had made them and which was showing through the lines of their poems like light through cracks in a wall, and Spanish, the language itself, which I learned so as to read the originals. It was the Spanish-language poetry that influenced my work, although I found some of the Latin American authors more congenital. I loved, of course, Garcia Lorca, especially his *Poeta en Nueva York*, as well as Rafael Alberti, Vicente Alexaindre, Miguel Hernandez, and of the generation of '98, Antonio Machado.

But I was also influenced significantly by Latin-American prose writers—first of all by García Márquez, but also by Alejo Carpentier, Juan Rulfo (his *Pedro Páramo* is a truly great work), and Miguel Angel Asturias. I liked Borges, but his aim of playing with the reader's mind, was foreign to my goals.

When did you "discover" these poets?

Oh, this was all within a year or so after I came to the US, so a round 1953, when I was 19. It was through the US public libraries, as I mentioned earlier.

What do you like more in their poetry?

71

Yuriy Tarnawsky

It's their way of speaking about the world, translating reality into images that expand and blossom in the reader's mind through associations. I call this a non-rational way of expressing yourself (I am avoiding "irrational" because of its negative connotations), which is identical to what the French Surrealists were doing, except I feel that their approach was artificial, prompted by Freud's theories, and in my opinion less successful, whereas the Hispanic one organic, based on the agelong tradition of folklore which is found in all cultures.

I think that my writing falls into the latter category, as does the work of some of the poets of the Ukrainian émigré avant-garde New York Group which I helped found. Also, the same can be said of some of other contemporary Ukrainian poetry, especially that of the members of the so-called Kyiv School. I think it's wonderful that poetry written in my native language appears to be related to what used to give me so much joy when I was starting out on my literary career. It was my aim to make it be like that.

What do you think about the political, and sometimes also ideological, engagement of many Latin-American poets, including Neruda?

Mixing anything with politics is dangerous, and you have to be very careful what you do. I tried doing it in my book-length poem *U ra na*, attempting to make it fully personal. I don't know how successful I was, but critics have observed that it is differed from many other Ukrainian patriotically-minded works. Shevchenko, I think, was surprisingly successful in this. Neruda sometime is, but much of his wring of this genre doesn't measure up to his early, individual poetry.

I love Pasolini's fiction, but can't say the same of his poetry. In fact, what I've seen of it, it doesn't look to me like poetry at all.

First published in Italian translation as "Lorenzo Pompeo intrevista a Jurij Tarnavs'kyj" in Poetarum Silva, *July, 2021.*

Lorenzo Pompeo is an Italian editor and translator.

INTERVIEW WITH GEORGE SALIS

GS: You were one of the founding members of the New York Group, a group of avant-garde Ukrainian diaspora writers. Can you reflect on your experiences with this group and what resulted from it? Can you tell us about some of the other writers who were involved in it?

YT: I arrived in this country in 1952, at the age of 18, and settled in Newark, NJ, across the river from Manhattan, which I started to visit on weekends practically from day one. There was a large Ukrainian community there (around 40,000 people), with a vibrant cultural life, centered around the Ukrainian Literary and Arts Club located at E. 9th St. and 2nd Ave., catty-corner from where the popular Ukrainian restaurant Veselka is now. There I became friends with a bunch of young Ukrainian artists and writers and participated in various events, which constituted sort of an informal artistic and literary movement. On Saturday, December 20, 1958, while having coffee at the Peacock Café on W. 4th St. near 6th Ave. (there is a Vietnamese noodle shop located there now), my writer friend Bohdan Boychuk, my wife Patricia (PN Warren), and I decided to start publishing a poetry journal *Novi Poeziji (New Poetry)* and to call ourselves the New York Group (NYG). Other young Ukrainian writers, from the U.S. as well as from other countries in the West, were invited to join in, and our membership, first being 6, over the years grew to 12. In addition

74

to the three of us (PN Warren adopted the penname Patricia Kilina), in the original group there were E. Vasylkivska, B. Rubchak, and E. Andiyevska. W. Wowk, O. Kowerko, Yu. Kolomiyets, M. Tsarynnyk, M. Rewakowicz, and R. Babowal joined the group later over a stretch of a number of years. The goal of NYG was to modernize Ukrainian literature, especially its poetry, by forcing it to shed its traditional, neo-romantic poetics and replacing its socially-oriented, often patriotic themes with those dealing with the burning existential issues of the contemporary urban man. A yearly publication, *New Poetry* came out over fourteen years (1969-1972), publishing almost exclusively free-verse original works and translations of the works of the icons of Modernism. After Ukraine's independence, 1990-1999, the group, in cooperation with the Writers' Union of Ukraine, published in Ukraine a quarterly literary journal *Svito-Vyd*. Since then, it has ceased its activities, although some of the members continue being active as individuals. In all, over the years, the group and its members are responsible for over 200 publications. While teaching at Columbia, I was able to help found the archive of NYG at the University's Rare Book and Manuscript Library, to which I contributed my papers. In 1996, we had a big inaugural opening of the archive with, as I recall, something like six, 4'x36' exhibit space.

NYG is a unique phenomenon not only in Ukrainian literature but apparently also in that of the whole Slavic world in that its primary influence comes from Hispanic poetry. The works of many of its members show a strong affinity with Existentialism and often bear the features of Surrealism. I think it would also be proper to view it as a U.S. phenomenon akin to the Yiddish theater in the U.S. in the first half of the 20th century—a Ukrainian contribution to American culture.

The following is from the jacket copy of your novel Three Blondes and Death: "Based on a complex mathematical scheme that the author, a computer scientist and linguist, developed as a substitute for the traditional architecture of a novel, and written in a deliberately sparse and structured syntax that ruthlessly compartmentalizes reality, Three Blondes and Death is an hermetic and hypnotic treatment of the classic themes of love and death." Could you go into some depth about this complex mathematical scheme? Have you applied your computer scientist knowledge to other aspects of your work? Would you say that these techniques are an extension of the Oulipian tradition?

The label "complex mathematical formula" is a bit misleading. It was the publisher's idea, and for some reason I didn't object to it. Let me explain what lies behind it. The rebellious spirit that I was at the time (1970), I wanted to write a novel which was not based on a plot, like virtually all novels that were written around me. But I had to have some other criterion on which to organize it. It was to be the story of a man and his love for three blondes and the simultaneous, unceasing drift toward death, so I decided to tell it in four separate parts. Hence 4 became a crucial factor in the book. With it in hand, I proceeded as follows. I wanted to break up the text into relatively short, autonomous sections. So, 40 appeared to be a reasonable choice. But having four parts with forty chapters each would have looked too uninteresting, too predictable. Besides, like the old weavers of Persian rugs who made deliberate errors in their masterpieces so as not to look too uppity in the eyes of Allah by aiming at being perfect, I decided to add 1 to the number of chapters in each part. I also didn't want to anger him by pretending to be infallible. But having four 41s would likewise have looked too predictable and perhaps uppity, so I decided to add 1 to the first and the second digit, in other words, 11 to the number of chapters in part four, bringing the total number of chapters to 52. So, now 4 appears to have disappeared from the book. But 41+41+41+52=175, and 1+7+5=13, and 1+3=4, which, presto, is the magic number! Yet it's hidden so far deep that maybe Allah, who is so busy with the daily affairs of the universe, will not notice it. I revert to using 4 also in other ways throughout the book, but it'd be too involved to discuss it here.

As I recall, I had read about Oulipo prior to writing *Three Blondes and Death* (*TBD*), but thought of it as a collaborative effort of a bunch of French writers, analogous to the collective French mathematical textbook authors known as Nicolas Bourbaki. Besides, they seemed to me to be engaged in writing something like sonnets, which was foreign to my intentions. It was only after *TBD* came out and I was talking about the book with Ron Sukenick at his place, with the book on the coffee table before us, that I learned from him more about them. As I recall, we talked then about the importance of form in a literary work, agreeing that form doesn't contribute to the quality of a work, but that every good literary work needs a form. In other words, there are no good or bad forms, but whatever form is chosen, it must be strictly adhered to. Oddly enough, I still didn't think at that time of *TBD* as being written in the restrictive mode, which it definitely is, not only because of relying on numerology, but especially because of the rigid grammar restrictions of the English in which it is composed. It was only after I met Jacques Roubaud and Marcel Benabou during their 2012 visit to the U.S. that I realized what I did was the same as what the Oulipians were doing. I gave them *TBD* as well as *Meningitis*, which is written in the same kind of restricted language, but they didn't show any interest in them.

I appear to be somewhat strange in that I like both numbers and words, that is, mathematics and literature. In my writing, I devote as much effort to form as to language. Studying engineering was not a fluke, but a calculated choice I made, knowing where it would lead me. I feel I would not be the writer that I am, had I chosen a different profession. But studying engineering didn't plant these traits in me, it merely made them more proficient. I have composed a little half-page document I call "Self-definition,"* which I sometimes read in public, in which among other things I say, "Writing for me is akin to proving a theorem—the goal is to do it, and do it as elegantly as possible." So, perhaps I should say that, as a writer, I was influenced by my technical background primarily by the methodology I learned there by applying it to my literary endeavors.

You've worked as a computer scientist at IBM Corporation, specializing in natural language processing and artificial intelligence. How do you feel about computer-generated creative works, such as novels, poetry, and even digital paintings? In general, do you think we have to worry about an apocalyptic scenario involving artificial intelligence?

I think it's fine to use computers as tools for producing artistic works, be it literature, film, music, or the plastic arts, but I don't think they will ever replace the human author. Computers can produce fine images and music, where patterns play an important role, but they cannot compete with people in arts that deal with emotions, such as literature. As long as there is no automaton that experiences the existential issues of a human being, no machine will be able to produce works that equal those written by a person. Such works can have great form, but will not project the emotional power associated with a well-written work.

Yuriy Tarnawsky

There is a danger, though, that AI will have a destructive influence on literature, and that one day computers will churn out poems, short stories, novels, etc., on-demand, satisfying the needs of the market. I can't help remembering the scary effectiveness of the early AI program ELIZA, which through simple parroting was able to fool people that they were talking to a human being. But, with the advances that have been made in the field, and even more so with those that are coming, the damage can be much greater. I'm saying "can," but should say "will." I don't know how we should fight against this, but I know that we must.

Your work at IBM involved a first-of-its-kind Russian-to-English automatic translation project. You've also translated works yourself. Are you of the mind that nothing is untranslatable?

I think everything is translatable, but not always with the same success. In cases where form and content—phonetics and semantics, that is, words and meanings—are inextricably linked, such as in some instances of poetry, it may be virtually impossible to produce an adequate translation and instead something vaguely related may have to be created. Part of this problem may lie in the culture in which the source and the target language exist, making the problem even more difficult. But such cases are relatively rare. So, one can say that, practically speaking, everything is translatable, although some works more easily and more successfully than others.

If you could have one of your works translated into every language, which would you choose and why?

Hmmm.... That's a difficult question. Can I say, all? I'm of a mind that all of my works are roughly of the same quality and I seem to like them all equally well (or badly), as I would with children if I had many. But I am probably wrong on this. Anyway, my answer—at one time I would have said, *Three Blondes and Death*, because of its size (some 250,000 words, and 450 pages) and the amount of time it took me to write it (more than twenty years), and also because of its radical nature, but now I will probably opt for *The Placebo Effect Trilogy,* partly also because of its size (some 150,000 words, and 700 pages), but also because of its nature. As you know, the trilogy consists of three books of five *mininovels* each, which are short works of fiction, whose effect is aimed to be that of a full-length novel. The genre is my own invention, and I think it is of some promise. Furthermore, with the trilogy, we are dealing with something close in aim if not in achievement to Balzac's *La Comédie humaine.* There are something like one hundred characters in it. I should mention that by "placebo effect" I mean Man's innate faith in his future, his will to live, which makes him fight on in the face of his always near, inevitable, and all-erasing end. In other words, it is a work dealing with the essential issues of Man's existence.

Yuriy Tarnawsky

What is a novel you've read and think deserves more readers?

I've been reading recently Roberto Bolaño's huge posthumous opus *2666,* and it would be nice if I would recommend it, but in all honesty, I can't. It's been praised to high heaven as being on the level with Márquez' masterpieces, but, in my opinion, it is a work overpowering not in its mastery, but in its size. True, the amount of detail it carries is overwhelming, but the links connecting the various parts are tenuous and contrived, and, most crucially, its final, fifth part seems to me to be badly out of kilter, completely foreign to the preceding parts, as if written by a different, much less talented author. Bolaño was seriously ill when he was completing the book, which may be the cause of this, but you don't get a pass on an exam because you're sick.

I would recommend, however, the work of another Latin-American writer, one which Márquez considered his master, the novel *Pedro Páramo* by the Mexican writer Juan Rulfo. I read it in the original back in the 1960's, soon after it came out, and it left a profound effect on me. I reread it last year and found it to be as powerful as before. It is a masterpiece, not to be missed. I think it is barely known in the U.S.

Your entire Placebo Effect Trilogy *is comprised of what you call "mininovels." [About them Joseph McElroy said: "Tarnawsky's are the second opinions we seek, almost recognize, then do, for they are made of the sounds, power sources, bizarre jobs, people coming our way, fitted together both by us and a culture by turns demanding and uncaring if we sleepwalkers notice or not: alarming, intelligent, caught again and again in the grasp of the author's surprise and yearning."] Have you thought of working on the opposite, gigantostories? Or is there a fractal effect involved with The* Placebo Effect Trilogy *as a whole?*

I presume, by "fractal effect" you mean repetition or replication of patterns. In that sense, no. I came up with the idea of the mininovel while working on the book of short stories *Short Tails* around 1997. I hadn't written any fiction for a long time and was having a whale of a time trying out different forms. One of them was a series of short chapters with gaps in time between them when important things must have happened, but which are not described, thus forcing the reader to come up with his own explanation of what and how this took place. I call these gaps "negative text," by analogy with "negative space" for "void" in cubist sculpture. Works like that, typically 15-30 pages long, when read, leave an aftereffect similar to that of having read a full-length novel. This happens because the reader has supplied his own information in order to properly perceive the work, becoming by this a co-author, together with the author of the mininovel. It's a very rewarding genre, and I have written seventeen such pieces in total—fifteen in *The Placebo Effect Trilogy,* and two in the collection *Crocodile Smiles.*

Yuriy Tarnawsky

But "gigantostories"—I think that's what novels are, right? Especially the big ones, like Tolstoy's *War and Peace* (I have heard it's been renamed recently to *Special Operation and Peace* in Russian), Pynchon's *Gravity's Rainbow*, Bolaño's *2666*, etc.

Your essay collection Claim to Oblivion *deals with theoretical issues of literature, particularly language use. How would you summarize the overarching thesis of that collection? What about your creative writing manual,* Literary Yoga*?*

Claim to Oblivion is a collection of essays and interviews that were written over many years, in which I talk about literary issues of special interest to me, many connected with my own writing, so there isn't in it one particular topic or viewpoint I focus on. But in general, in keeping with my nature, it is a series of arguments against the traditional view of writing.

In *Literary Yoga* I tried to sum up everything I have learned about writing over some sixty years and offer it for free (that is, for the piddling 16 dollars the publisher charges for the book) to anyone who wants to make use of it. I wouldn't have given my arm and leg for it, but gladly would have signed over all of my royalties for the next ten years for a book like this when I was starting out to write. It would have saved me a lot of grief. It consists of a series of exercises the aim of which is to point out to the user the various choices at his disposal as he is composing and the effects these produce. The book is subtitled "Exercises for Those Who Can Write," and may be used as a textbook or a self-study manual.

This is a guest question from Max Nestelieiev: "Dear, Yuriy. What does it mean for you to write in different languages? Do you feel them differently? And what are the main advantages of the English language compared to Ukrainian?" I would also like to know how you would compare and contrast the English language with the Ukrainian language in general.

Oh, it's nice Maxym is with us. I enjoyed so much working with him on the translation of *Warm Arctic Nights*. He did a terrific job, and I am grateful for him having taken on that difficult task and having been so receptive to my suggestions, in particular, when I wanted to use more archaic language from Western Ukraine before the Russian occupation. I think we came up with a beautiful, organic amalgam of the past and the present.

As to the question—is it different for me to write in different languages? I have to reply in a strange way—yes and no. I think I'm equally proficient in both languages, and when I write, I seem not to feel any difference. But that must be only on the surface. I must associate different things with the word equivalents in the two languages, and as I write, I suspect, they pull me in different directions. These associations are partly what's called in linguistics "semantic fields," but also undoubtedly personal associations, conditioned by individual experience. So, when I choose to write in one language or the other, I must be deciding to write two different works—works similar on one level, but different on another. It's a very thorny issue and is only partly explainable by the Saphir-Whorf Hypothesis, which maintains that speakers of different languages think differently because of the different languages they use.

There are advantages of writing in English because through it I have a vastly bigger audience. But also, I have drifted away from Ukrainian after having lived practically all my life in foreign-language environments, and am not as comfortable with the vocabulary, especially one dealing with everyday objects that have come into use within, say, the past fifty years.

I have completely different feelings about the two languages as I write in them—Ukrainian seems delicate and beautiful, like a fine China cup of translucent porcelain, and also, oddly enough, like a glass of crystal-clear water. English is chewy and pliable like a big wad of gum, or, better, of wood resin I am masticating as I build sentence after sentence, feeling its texture and savoring its redolent taste. I have noticed that sometimes I even move my jaws and tongue and swallow as I write, without being conscious of it, as if I was actually chewing on the words. English is God's gift to humanity, and I am grateful to him for it.

I've seen people posting photos of Ukrainian fiction that they're now reading. I've also noticed some publishers offering deals on the Ukrainian fiction they've published. Do you think this is an example of "slacktivism" or is there something of depth there? What is the best way for people to help during the current war?

I think it's just people cashing in. They see the market potential and want to take advantage of it. But I hope the aftereffect will stay on.

What do you say to people on the internet who claim you've "abandoned" your country or that you're not Ukrainian because you've lived in the United States for so long?

Is that what they are saying? I have published a couple dozen books in Ukrainian. Have they bought any? I have two volumes of collected poems in Ukrainian that are out of print and no one wants to republish them. I got an offer from a publisher—he'll do it for $7,000 of my money, will keep 250 copies himself, and give me 250, to stick them up anything I want to. I can't think for the moment of a hole big enough for them to fit in, so I'm making him wait.

I feel actually extremely comfortable writing in English while being ready to step into Ukrainian whenever needed.

Yuriy Tarnawsky

What are some of your fondest memories of Ukraine?

Before the war. My father and mother young and healthy, I—a child, especially during summer vacations at my grandmother's. Part one of *Warm Arctic Nights.*

If you were in a room with Putin, what would you tell him?

Oh, I wouldn't talk to him at all, but would tackle him instantly to bring him down. He's a Judo expert and 18 years younger than me, but I was a marathon runner and used to be in great shape, and I'm sure I'd beat him as Ukraine is sure to beat Russia. Motivation, as everyone knows by now, means a lot–means at least three times as much as none.

I'd tie him up then and take him to Nuremberg, which is where the trials will once again be held and would attend his hanging, to which, I am sure, I would be invited.

But if I were to talk to him, I'd speak in profanities as you can speak only in Russian and as those twelve brave Ukrainian sailors on Snake Island spoke to the Russian flagship Moskva that soon thereafter was sunk by Ukrainian rockets, when they were ordered to surrender, saying, *"Russkij korabl', poshel nakhuj!"* [Russian ship, go fuck yourself!] So, I'd say, *"Russkij pizdjent, poshel nakhuj."* [Russian pussydent [actually much worse than that], go fuck yourself!"] I certainly wouldn't try to reason with him. He doesn't have a mind, just the reptilian brain.

You're working on a novel titled Sebastian in a Dream, *which you've said is "inspired by Georg Trakl's poem* 'Sebastian im Traum' *and patterned on J. S. Bach's* Goldberg Variations. *Can you reflect on this poetic impetus and tell us how the writing process has been unfolding, particularly in relation to the musical structure? When can we expect to see it published?*

Bach is the pinnacle of mastery for me and the *Variations* one of the finest instances of it, and Trakl is one of my two favorite poets, the second one being Rimbaud, and *"Sebastian im Traum"* is my favorite poem of his. I followed the aria-thirty variations-aria pattern of the *Variations* in the novel, and used the beginning of the *poem "Mutter trug das Kindlein im weißen Mond"* [Mother carried the little child in a white moon] as the phrase for the aria, and then bounced off it thirty times. It'd be too involved to say more about it. It was the most difficult book I did since *TBD.* It's finished, and I have a publisher or two looking at it, but haven't really started looking for one seriously. I have in the meantime started to work on another novel, a potential companion to *Sebastian in a Dream,* based on one of El Greco's paintings. I don't know if it's going to pan out so I'd rather not say anything more about it.

Yuriy Tarnawsky

* Self-definition:

For me writing is a highly personal endeavor, an existential act, through which I am able to be myself—I write, therefore I am.

Although there is virtually no raw autobiographical data in my writing, all of it deals with subjects and themes that occupy me and which have been stirred up by the events in my life. I am a very private person and feel uncomfortable disclosing to others the details of my biography. Besides, imagination is so much more powerful than everyday life; compare the incredible—scary or exhilarating— experiences we live through in our dreams at night, to the drab events we trudge through in the daytime. It is for this reason I frequently turn to dreams in my writing. They enable me to create more effective works, with greater impact on the reader.

My technical background has had a profound impact on my writing, causing me to devote much attention to language and form. I am not concerned with how readers will react to my work. Writing for me is akin to proving a theorem—the goal is to do it, and do it as elegantly as possible.

Yuriy Tarnawsky – February 17, 2015

First published as "Literary Theorems: An Interview with Yuriy Tarnawsky," *The Collidescope, June 12, 2022.*

George Salis is an American author and blogger.

INTERVIEW WITH JUSTINA DOBUSH

YT: One of the best decisions I ever made was to study linguistics. It changed my life. I used to love arguing when I was young. I wanted to set everyone straight. In the '50's, in New York, my friends and I argued every time we got together, and I did it particularly stubbornly. But then, when I finished my doctorate, I completely lost interest in arguing. I thought, I can say what I think, but you think differently, so, go ahead, think differently. I don't care if you're right or wrong, because if you don't know something and you speak nonsense, it's your choice. But if you know something better than me, that's fine too. Maybe I should change my mind. It fundamentally changed my personality. I have noticed that people are often unpleasant not because they are bad by nature, but because they think of themselves as different than what they are and they think that they have to fight for things that are important to them. It often gets them into trouble.

JD: It is better to just be yourself and not pay attention to other people or try to match their level, not to fight with them, but rather to fight with yourself.

That's right, and my doctorate helped me to realize this.

You have repeatedly spoken about the decline of literature. For me it is also crucially important to understand what is happening with reading now. Especially here in Ukraine, we have a lot of complaints that people don't read and we have to promote reading. Although, in my opinion, the problem is not how much we read but whether we read at all. After all, many people have lost the understanding of what reading is in general, consequently turning it into an end in itself. In your opinion, do we need to talk more about what reading is and what it means?

I think that forcing people to read is not the way to go. It won't help. Maybe it'll even be better to have fewer readers, if they are better readers, so to speak. After all, why do people nowadays read less in general? Because what used to be available in a book can now be found on TV, in a computer, and so on, and it satisfies their primitive daily needs. But if you are a person of a different caliber, a different type, and you need a good book, then you should have such a book available to you. We need to create good literature for people of this type and somehow promote the emergence of such, perhaps smaller groups of readers, so they can get something useful from reading. And why do you need such literature? Because with the help of art–and literature is part of it– you discover things that tell you about the essence of life, about the essence of being human, the essence of the world, which will never be produced by commercial writers. And you, as a noncommercial writer, meet the needs of those people. Because most of the people who are interested in commercial literature, who are interested in TV, etc., they will not read good literature anyway. They don't want it because it bores them and doesn't satisfy their needs. They need commercial literature, and the society has to give it to them because otherwise they will look for it elsewhere, in other languages. (I am thinking of Ukraine, which had reasonably good literature but very little commercial, and Ukrainian readers had to look for it among the literature of their neighbors, such as Russia and Poland, who were not positively disposed toward Ukraine. As a result, Ukrainian readers were supporting their potential enemies.) Nevertheless, it is necessary for good literature to exist in parallel with the commercial for a core of high culture to be formed around it, uniting at the same time part of the society around it.

And if we talk about the writing itself, you are constantly experimenting with language, text and genre. In your opinion, why are so few writers trying to experiment today and choose a commercialized approach to creating their own texts instead? Doing so, don't they deprive themselves of individuality and originality? Why are we so reluctant to express ourselves?

Why does one write? I write because I need to express myself, because I fight with my inner demons, the dragons of my life, on the pages of my manuscripts. I do it as if proving a theorem, and I want to find the simplest and most elegant way to do it. But most writers don't write like that. They write because they want to be famous, they want to have an impact on the society, they want to be loved, and, of course, they write because they want to make money. This is the reason why we in Ukraine have pretty good commercial literature today but relatively scarce pure literature. I don't want to criticize contemporary Ukrainian writers because I don't know them well enough and they have the right to do what they want. Some of them do write well, but it seems to me that they are not immune to commercialism enough to neglect the tastes of the readers and the requirements of the publishers to make their works as good as they could be.

When it comes to writing, it is commonly accepted that a writer should know the language he writes in, have a rich vocabulary, and in general manage the language expertly. So, shouldn't a better knowledge of the language lead to better literature?

I find this hard to agree with. I fought against the "rich vocabulary" theory from the beginning. I see no reason why it is necessary to have a large vocabulary to write well. After all, if you don't know how to use words correctly, it doesn't matter how many you know. You can use few words, but in a good way, or vice versa—use a lot of words badly. And even exceptional knowledge of the language in general will not make you a good writer, because being a writer is something innate, and it exists to a large extent beyond language, and for instance, plays an important role in cinematography. For example, one of the greatest Ukrainian writers and probably the best Ukrainian prose writer, Vasyl

Stefanyk, wrote with a very limited vocabulary and in a dialect to boot. His language was restricted, but his works are written with such skill that it is difficult for me to name someone better than him among Ukrainian prose writers.

I think in order to be a good writer, you must, first of all, have a strong, confident personality, second, reject all unnecessary external influences, and proceed with your work as if proving a theorem. But if you want your books to sell well, then you should look at the bestsellers, check what topics publishers are looking for, write something like that, and maybe add your own dose of sex and scandal. But this will not be literature. High art is like mathematics—there are certain rules and conventions in it and you must follow them the same way as a mathematician observes the rules and conventions of mathematics while proving a theorem.

What is your view on Creative Writing programs? To what extent can a writer figure out on his own the rules and conventions that will help him improve his writing?

Just think of how many wonderful writers we have that came before the middle of the third quarter of the 20th century without the existence of Creative Writing programs. Shakespeare also didn't go to school to learn how to write plays. You can learn everything on your own, and that's great, because then only those who have the greatest need and have the most to say, will develop themselves. I go to conferences of various writers' associations, and in some of them there may up to 40,000 people, of whom 10,000 may be writers and the rest students, or rather mostly female students. Who needs thousands of new writers a year? And how can they be unique when they are taught what to do? I remember how I once went to a lecture at one of these conferences and there was someone talking about plot, how it should be structured, and that there should be the main plot, and the secondary one, and maybe even the third one.... Lord! I got up and walked out. And soon after that in a fit of rage I wrote an article on how useful it is to break a rule. Yes, rules exist to be broken, and when you're taught that you have to follow the rules, it's very difficult to even want to break them, let alone doing it. I think it would be better if all those Creative Writing programs didn't exist. I don't see any need for them. Why do we need hundreds of thousands of writers instead of only hundreds who are able to create good works of literature? Because that number is enough, even by US standards, to produce enough books to meet all publishing and cultural needs each year.

And the fewer spurious readers, the less frustration and pressure on the author, the less of a need to explain what was written to those people who in principle cannot understand it.

In America, there exist two different worlds of readers—one for the popular commercial writers, and one for the non-commercial ones, the first one is big, and the second one much smaller. I believe such a phenomenon awaits Ukraine in the future.

And how did it happen that you stopped liking Jean-Paul Sartre?

Gradually, over the years, I began to drift away from his philosophy. The main reason however was that I learned eventually what kind of person Sartre really was—that in some ways he was quite despicable on personal level, and in addition how ugly was his relationship with Simone de Beauvoir. She would send him her female students to sleep with, which he did. I used to like his works, but now I can't read them. Even *Nausea*, which is his best work, bores me. I feel the same about Camus even though I once admired his writing. Now it bores me and seems awkwardly written.

Sartre's literary works are an illustration of his philosophical musing. That's fine. I am not able to criticize him as a fellow, a philosopher would, but when someone tries to prove that there is no God, as he does in one of his articles, it comes across as childish. God has nothing to do with rationality. He's a belief, and it is impossible to prove that he exists or doesn't. He hasn't been defined as falsifiable. And, most importantly, God is a human need, something which a philosopher should understand. By the way, regarding this topic — I recently got myself, four of Richard Dawkins' books. I started reading the first one, but realized that it was complete garbage and dishonesty, so I put it away and shipped all four books back. He says that if there was no faith in God, we wouldn't have terrorist attacks by Muslims, the Inquisition, etc. This may be true, but he fails to mention that we also wouldn't have all those wonderful cathedrals and beautiful examples of art and music, and the holidays that we all love so much, and that children wouldn't have St. Nicholas and the gifts he brings, and so on, and so on. That is, there is another side to religion, and if you criticize it for the bad things, you should mention the good ones too. Moreover, these terrorist attacks are not a unique feature of religion, but also of political thinking. Let us recall communism and the purges of Stalin and Mao. What's more, even football teams have fans who attack others because of their enthusiasm for their team. Well, so how can someone who considers himself a thinker speak so dishonestly?

I once admired Sartre because he said there was no God, which is what I fervently thought myself. I continue thinking that there is no God, but that doesn't mean that on some level I don't need him or don't believe in him. Because, the same as others, I curse God for the evil things done to me he allegedly turns a blind eye to, and I pray to him when I need something. I think this kind of behavior is typical of all of us and that it is innate. So, I got disillusioned with Sartre's philosophy and his literary works. At the same time, as a result, I became better disposed toward to religion, just the rituals, though, not the dogma. I think that religious rituals are very effective. For example, when you go to a priest and tell him your sins, and he forgives you, and you believe in it, it must be a wonderful cleansing. And then consider the various liturgies, and the ringing of bells, and the smell of incense, and the different rites, all of which has nothing to do with dogma—they're wonderful, and they bring joy into people's life, and it makes no sense to take it away from them. In fact, it is impossible. People don't listen to the evidence against religion because believing has nothing to do with reasoning. Such efforts are pointless because they are ineffective and there is no need for them. People need this formal part of religion, so why try to take it away from them?

I also see it the same way now—that it doesn't matter that God may not exists—you still need something to believe in.

Yes, it's true. Then the person finds something else to believe in instead of God, for instance, Marxism or Nazism, or racism — racism of different colors and shades. Although with racism it's a little different because I think it is in our genes to be drawn to those like ourselves, but it can be turned into something pernicious, when you not only love people like you, but hate the other ones. The feeling of belonging to a group, having a stake in this group, is part of being human.

Yuriy Tarnawsky

Returning to Sartre, today I finished the seventh draft of my latest novel, *Sebastian in a Dream*. This work was inspired by the poem *"Sebastian im Traum"* by the great Austrian poet Georg Trakl. I like him very much and it was he who inspired me to write this novel, although I based it formally on Bach's *Goldberg Variations*. That is, it consists of an aria, thirty variations, and the repetition of the aria. I finished it sometime in early June of 2021, but I made some changes and the current version is probably the final one, and it happens to be the seventh. You know, Hohol said that for a work to be completed, it must be rewritten seven times, and being Ukrainian like Hohol, I followed his orders. In this work, among those thirty variations, there are four screams of anguish that are invectives against God for being so bad. This is not my real opinion, but just a conceit in the novel. There I talk about how terrible God is, and may he allow us to curse him and say all sorts of bad things in moments of despair, but at the end I excuse him because he is "a paraplegic of cosmic dimensions." Creation of the world was such an incredible effort that he collapsed and was able to create only a few of the parts from which to make the world. And he created them with the "little toe on his left foot" because of being paralyzed. That's why we shouldn't blame him for the world being so bad. In the novel, I speak of randomness as the substitution or manifestation of God. There is a cause for everything, and every effect must have it, and everything that exists is an effect of some cause. These are the laws that govern the world. And God is randomness. In the novel I express my view on the world, which is connected with my Existentialism and Sartre.

Is it possible to consider such an approach to God as a universal language that a writer can use? Isn't this the most universal way of conveying one's inner experiences?

I think that this belief in God has nothing to do with literature or art in general, because it is a characteristic of every human being and is encoded in our genes. I believe we have a need for God and the idea of afterlife because our brains have become too powerful. We can understand that our lives eventually come to an end and that we are nothing more than chemical compounds that combine into physical particles which eventually must decompose. But living with the understanding that you will die one day is very difficult, and that's why we have this need to believe in life after death, that there is someone who created us and that he did for a purpose. All our behavior is based on the realization that everything that happens must have a cause. Therefore, if we exist, someone must have created us. It is deeply rooted in each of us. A writer may or may not write about this—most don't and don't even give it any consideration, but I don't believe it can be considered a universal language of writing.

Isn't it risky to return to the theme of God in our secular world?

Yuriy Tarnawsky

Just being alive is risky, but you have no choice. When you feel the need to do something, you do it. By definition, there is no choosing here. I try to be honest with myself and am convinced that there is no afterlife, but somehow, I have accepted this fact and can still live more or less normally. But most people need to believe differently. Our body has simply generated this feeling of immortality, so that we can live on, for otherwise there'd be suicides all the time and all over the place, and in general the human race wouldn't have developed to the degree that it has.

When moving to the US, immigrants often become typical members of the diaspora who try to assimilate. That is, their tendency to try do shed their immigrant identity dominates every aspect of their activity. What prevented you from becoming such a person?

You know, there is a well-known fact in linguistics that small communities of people who have moved from their home country someplace else turn linguistically conservative. At a time when the language is changing in the mainland, it is preserved in those small islands among foreign languages. For example, there are some regions in America which have retained the features of English from the 16th century. The same is true of other spheres of behavior. Look at how powerful was the Ukrainian émigré community of the people who left Ukraine in 1944. These were patriots, educated people who contributed in a major way to the development of Ukrainian culture. I never thought I would stay in America. I thought my moving here was temporary, that we were working to create Ukraine there to bring it home. This is a normal phenomenon among conscious patriots. On the other hand, there are those who, for some reason, simply forget about their roots and assimilate. By the way, the Ukrainian diaspora has developed into one of the most powerful in America. It was and still is a very well-organized society. For example, such a phenomenon as the New York Group of Ukrainian writers doesn't have an equivalent among any other ethnic group here, or as far as I know, anywhere else in the world. This was due to the political situation and the fact that the Ukrainian immigrant community consisted mostly of the intelligentsia, which was a very important factor. But I have noticed that those Ukrainians who come to the United States now assimilate faster than we did. Five years ago, my wife and I were in Chicago and went to the Ukrainian Museum in the Ukrainian Village. There was an exhibition there from Ukraine and some newly arrived teenagers with Ukrainian roots milled around, already speaking English to each other instead of Ukrainian. When people of my generation came here, we spoke only Ukrainian among ourselves. That is, members of the current diaspora no longer feel a need to hold on to their Ukrainian identity. By the way, in Ukraine we can observe the same thing—there is still a large segment of the population who speak Russian. For me, this lack of need to be yourself is simply unthinkable. This is probably because the political system in which these people grew up was such that they don't need to be themselves. But I can't say that this is true of all who have recently come here.

Why is it important for you to remain part of the Ukrainian discourse?

Apparently, I'm inconsistent. I became very Ukrainian when the Chornobyl catastrophe happened and then I felt a strong need for my daughter to speak Ukrainian as well and to raise her as a Ukrainian in general. If I had children now, I would probably do the same, because I continue speaking Ukrainian even with my Polish wife. So, I still remain Ukrainian even though I write mostly in English. I just look at English as the lingua franca, as Latin once used to be.

But in what language do you dream? You know, as Taras Prokhasko once wrote in a column for Zbruc. *Do you see your dreams in Ukrainian still or are they in English already?*

Dreams have no language (*laughs*). Dreams are visual phenomena. When somebody speaks in a dream, it depends on who he is. If he's someone who normally speaks English, he'll speak English, and if he normally speaks Ukrainian, then he'll speak Ukrainian. Dreams undoubtedly are nothing but a product of our brain, our mind, and our dreams are what we are. If we belong to the Ukrainian culture, which has its own unique features, one of which is this irrationality, this oneiric quality which we see in the so-called "bizarre prose" of Hohol, Kvitka-Osnovyanenko and some later writers, then, say, an American, will not have the same kind of dreams as we, who are constantly confronted, with this dream-like outlook on life while conscious. But it's not about language, it's about the culture of the society you're belong to. However, I am not an expert on this subject and I may be wrong.

Are you still inspired by the cinema as you once used to be?

I used to love movies. When I was young, films had a huge influence on me, but now, unfortunately, the new cinema doesn't move me at all. I consider Dovzhenko to be a very important director, and I think Ukraine has produced some very interesting films. I don't know if Hollywood has made as many good films as Ukraine has. Hollywood has had some great actors, talented directors, and so on, but the goal of its films was always to make money, which didn't allow for artistically good films to be made. The tradition was also completely different.

Generally speaking, I don't find anything interesting in the movies any more. I am always looking for something good, but don't see anything. I think we need a crisis of some sort to come for things to change. We have to go back to simpler things. Plots, for instance, are now so confusing, but for what reason? You can have a simple plot and make a great film. These confusing plots don't make films better, but just the opposite.

So, in your opinion, plot is not essential in a movie?

No, I don't think it is, nor is it essential to literature. I intentionally made *Three Blondes and Death* plotless to prove my point. Look at it this way—you meet a person who becomes a close friend of yours, and over a long period of time you create a chronological image of his development in your mind, despite the fact that you received the information about him in a non-chronological order. However, you will have a correct idea of this person and will be able to reproduce even chronologically what life he's had. Similarly, in a work of art, you don't have to build up the story chronologically. You can present the facts in the order you wish, but when the reader finishes reading the book, he will still have a clear idea of what happened, having created the chronology on his own. Instead, you can build up your story in a different way, and if you organize the presentation in an interesting fashion, you will end up with something even better than if you'd based it on chronology.

In my new novel, as I have said, I have taken the form of Bach's variations as a canvas—I have thirty variations organized in a certain way and divided into ten subparts. Apart from that, I lay another pattern over them — I took the first four variations and I repeated them three times after every ninth variation. So, I take the same theme and vary it one way or another several times, and in addition perform some other variations. So, this is the scheme that I have chosen and it plays an important organizing role. Without it, the novel would be a jumbled mess.

Are you inspired by classical music?

Bach for me is the pinnacle of art. I have never studied music and am very sorry that I didn't. We were taught to read music in high school, although not well enough for me to sing off a printed page confidently now. But, from the beginning, I felt an organic attraction to Bach's music. And already in my first novel *Roads*, which I wrote in my 20's, there is a scene where a man hums a tune, and the protagonist first thinks it's Bach, but then realizers it is Mozart's *"Eine kleine Nachtmusik,"* and is disappointed by the discovery. It is interesting that even then, when I was 21, without any musical training, I felt that Bach is better than Mozart. And now, when I hear a classical music piece that has no counterpoint, I find it uninteresting. It's just that my ear feels that there's something missing. I used to love the music of the French composer François Couperin at one time, but now have no desire to hear it because it doesn't employ counterpoint. And, although its melodies are beautiful, it seems to me like it lacks something. When I detect counterpoint, my brain instantly latches onto it and delights in following along. I also like the music of the Middle Ages, especially religious works, the music of the Renaissance, because of its polyphony, and some music from the Baroque period. Bach, of course, is Baroque, but it is late Baroque and it is its highest achievement. I also love modern music—Stockhausen, Berio, Xenakis, Ligeti, Crumb, Toru Takemitsu, Salonen.

And nineteenth century, music of the Romantic period, it doesn't speak to you?
Well, for some reason, I find romanticism not to my liking. It strikes me as sentimental, even slobbery. I fight against the Romanticism in me all the time and don't want it to come out.

Why?

I don't know. I just think it's a bad trait. I think my writing isn't romantic at all. It's a conscious choice. My first book of poetry, for instance, is extremely dry, both in its content and the title—*Life in the City*. I changed a lot after that, I often turn to dreams, but I never became a romantic.

The worst thing a journalist can do is ask the interviewee "What inspires you?" But what do you think, especially when one speaks to a writer, is it appropriate to talk about inspiration, even though it says a lot about creativity, where it, come from and so on?

I think that inspiration is such an obscure and ill-defined term that you can interpret in many different ways, much as you can interpret the concept of love. Love is the most misinterpreted word in the world, because everyone understands it differently. As to inspiration, I agree that there must be some impetus for creating. I have talked about my new novel, *Sebastian in a Dream,* inspired by Georg Trakl's poem of the same title, although there is almost nothing connecting the two except for the phrase I chose from the poem, "mother carried the little child in a white moon." But in my case the inspiration was primarily rational. In general, I just have the need to write – it is probably a habit at my age. However, different people may be inspired by totally different things.

Are you afraid that time will come when nothing will inspire you or give an impetus to writing?

You know, in the last poem in my first book, I say that I will keep on writing until I become so happy that I will no longer write. The point is that I am waiting to say everything I have to say and will have nothing left. To some extent, I think the same now: It will be wonderful if I no longer have a need to write because writing is an incredible torment—it brings the writer pleasure, but at the same time, it is still a torment. On the other hand, although I am not really afraid of that, I still think, "God, what will I do if I no longer write"?" I will probably be climbing walls then and will obviously be a different person. But maybe then everything will be fine. It all

Yuriy Tarnawsky

depends on how much time I have left. To be honest, I don't think that it's that much.

First published Iin APOFENIE, June 27, 2022.
Translated by Yulia Lyubka, edited by Yuriy Tarnawsky

Justina Dobush is a Ukrainian journalist

CRAFT MAGAZINE INTERVIEW WITH OLEKSANDR MYMRUK

OM: When we planned to have this conversation over a year ago, the world around us was completely different, although there was a sense of impending major changes in the air. The world before 2022 was dominated by the pandemic, people wearing masks, discussions about climate, and plans for the next year... And then, on the 24th of February, everything changed, and I think the questions the writers answer now are very different from those before. So, what can we say about Ukrainian writers? Could you tell me Yuriy, what you are currently being asked in interviews? Have literary questions taken a back seat?

YT: I think that since then, I have had two interviews. One of them was a conversation with George Salis. He has a website called *The Collidescope,* and we talked about literature there, and then he asked me what I would say to Putin if we met. I replied that I wouldn't say anything to him but would simply throw myself at him, tackle him, tie him up, and take him to Nuremberg, and that I would probably be invited to witness his hanging there. It's impossible to talk to Putin. He doesn't think, he just reacts to his reptilian brain.

Every day I check to see what's happening in Ukraine. At first, I was afraid, and thought that it would be over for us very soon, but then euphoria set in and I began to feel that we would win. But now I have a feeling that it might turn into a long, drawn-out stalemate which would be very bad for Ukraine. It's better for Russia— they have vast resources. We can see now that the imposed sanctions are not working as well as expected. So, I'm quite concerned about the situation. People often say that a Ukrainian counteroffensive will start soon and the war will end, but I'm not optimistic about it, although I am convinced that in the end, we will win. However, I think it will be a very bloody and costly war.

If the Russians can indeed continue for a long time.

By the way, I have stopped calling them Russians. For me, they are Muscovites. Until the beginning of the 18th century, they referred to themselves as the "Muscovite State." Then Peter the Great Son of a Bitch, renamed it Russia, and it was a huge blow to Ukraine. They appropriated our vast culture and history and made it their own. We must put an end to this right away.

Have you heard about the petition that has gathered over 20,000 signatures calling for the official renaming of Russia to Muscovy? It has already been submitted for the president for consideration.

I saw that just yesterday. It's interesting to think if I had anything to do with it because a video recently appeared online where I argue that Russia is not Russia but "Muscovy. Perhaps it influenced someone's opinion. I would be very glad if it did.

You have never been associated with the image of a poet who writes so-called civic poetry, and there are not many such texts in your work. However, during 2022, I came across fragments from your poems "Ukraine," "Russia," as well as the poem Urana. Your readers especially like to mention your image of Ukraine as a "chewed-up heart." But you didn't stop there and have recently written a poem called "It is the rotting of the corpse," which deals with the war. You read it in front of American audience. How did they react?

I initially wrote this poem in English and have subsequently translated it into Ukrainian, and it came out in *Ukrajina Moloda*, as "*Ce hnyje trup*." It was written specifically for City of Asylum Pittsburgh (a nonprofit organization, that helps writers exiled from their countries, offering them free housing, medical services, and other assistance in the United States). The organization operates in several cities in addition to Pittsburgh. When invited to perform, I initially thought of reading something from *Urana*, but I felt the need to write something new, and this is what came out. The poem was conceived as an op-ed piece, like a letter to the editor of a newspaper (I was thinking in particular of *The New York Times.*) It was recently published in the original in *Kyiv Post*.

Yuriy Tarnawsky

As to the reaction, it was very positive. I got a standing ovation. Afterwards, some people came up to me and express their praise. I've heard from other Americans that this poem resonated with them.

When it was published in *Ukrajina Moloda*, Yuriy Kovaliv, the poet and literary critic, posted a link to it on Facebook, and there were some Ukrainian readers who didn't like it. (I remember a comment from some female reader, saying, "But I didn't like it!"). How can you talk about liking or disliking an op-ed piece which lays out the facts? This is a work intended to draw attention to what is happening, not to please someone's esthetic sensibilities. I don't live in Ukraine, and I don't see what's happening there, but I write what I know from the media, and so I conveyed it in the form I received it in. I feel that the poem accomplishes what it sets out to do—to evoke a boundless, justified hatred for Russia. So, I'm surprised by Ukrainian readers' reactions. It appears that foreigners react to it more properly.

I think I ought to mention at this point that the poem is written in Whitmanesque poetics, in that it is structured on anaphora, in other words, repetition of the initial phrase, something Whitman often employed, as for instance in the famous "I Hear America Singing." I did this deliberately, wanting to point out by this my dual indebtedness—that to my Ukrainian heritage and to my American citizenship. This fact, by the way, was noticed by some non-

Ukrainians who have heard me read the piece, but not by Ukrainians. In October of 2022, for instance, I read the poem in Madrid, at the magnificent Madrid Ateneo building, interspersed with a Spanish-language translation by Alain Arias-Misson, and was gratified to near that some in the audience had picked it up.

I worked on *Urana* for about a year and a half or two. It was an incredibly painful task. The piece is not just a poem—it's a book some 150 pages long. I worked on it right after Chornobyl, when I realized for the first time that Ukraine was disappearing, that it might soon cease to exist, and so I wrote in a paroxysm of despair. Some people then also told me that they didn't like the poem. My poetry has always been based on metaphors, and in this poem, just as in "It is the rotting of the corpse," I rely more on rhetorical devices, so they sound different, but nevertheless, I think they are effective in the way they are intended to be.

I wrote the poem "Ukraine" in 1965, after returning from Spain. When you look at the map, the shape of Ukraine is very similar to a traditionally depicted heart which has been chewed up, so I used this metaphor in the poem. And "Russia" was written in 1970 as a reaction to the suppression of the "Prague Spring," when Soviet planes landed at Prague airport one morning. These poems are over 50 years old, but to me, they are just as relevant today.

Yuriy Tarnawsky

I would like to write something personal about this war, but I can't. I'm not there, and I can only experience it through the news I hear. That's why "It is the rotting of the corpse" turned out the way it did.

There is currently a real explosion of civic and military poetry in Ukraine. Poets, as always, are the first among all artists to react to current events. There is even a special website now dedicated to collecting such poems, and the anthologies of Ukrainian poetry abroad are countless. Undoubtedly, these poems vary in quality, but still, what do you think—can civic poetry truly have an impact? Or is it rather a tool for self-therapy for the author, a way to explain something to oneself?

I am saddened by what I have seen. Most of the works I have read are weak, beginners' pieces that are extolled as poetic masterpieces. I don't know, maybe there are good works out there somewhere, but I haven't come across any that moved me poetically. Perhaps it's therapy, but in many cases, I believe it is primarily self-promotion. People are rushing in with their work to publishing houses with the same fervor as they used to with their peans to the "great brotherly Russian people" and the "democratic, humanitarian communism" in the Soviet times. The similarity is frightening. It's clear, everyone is trying to cash in.

I obviously haven't read everything and don't want to mention any names, but I am really saddened by what's happening. I used to bemoan the fact that traditional verse was still being written in Ukraine, and now almost everyone has switched to free verse, but the poems are no better. At least back then, one could hide behind the form, but now everything is exposed, revealing its rickety essence. It seems like this is nothing more than an attempt to join in, become popular, and gain fame.

Did you ever think, Yuriy, that you would have to live through times of great change again? You have a rich life experience. I remember in 2019 when you presented the Ukrainian translation of the novel Warm Polar Nights. *It was a text precisely about life at a turning point—war, occupation, and a huge flood of refugees to Europe. All of this applies to the current situation, and we know that there are already thousands of Ukrainian children who have experiences similar to yours.*

I never thought that this would happen. While I feared that Putin might do something, I didn't expect it to reach this level. The destruction, devastation of cities and the environment—I believe such a war has never been seen before, except perhaps in Vietnam. I don't understand how Ukraine will rebuild, how long it will take for it to happen, and given my age, I don't think I will live to see what it will look like in the end. It's a unique war, where one great nation attacks another and says, "You don't have the right exist, we Will destroy you."

Yuriy Tarnawsky

This morning I learned that a documentary film about Navalny received an Oscar award, but not the film about Ukrainian children from the frontline territories, "A House Made of Splinters." At first, I thought, well, it's alight, it's about Navalny who's against Putin, but Navalny himself recently said that Crimea is Russia and that it should not be returned.

He said that Crimea is not a sandwich that can be passed back and forth.

Well, you see. Now, it seems like he changed his mind, but I don't believe in Russian liberalism.

While everything in Ukraine has become engulfed in the war and has pushed aside other news, you managed to start another novel after completing Sebastian in a Dream. *If we consider this work as another reflection of your experience, what does it tell us?*

I started writing it towards the end of 2021, anticipating what was about to happen. And with the outbreak of the war, it became a cozy place for me, where I could hide and protect myself from the horrific news that came day after day. The title of the novel is "The Burial of the Count of Orgaz," taken from one of El Greco's finest paintings located in the small church of Santo Tomé in the Spanish city of Toledo. I have just finished the first draft, and if all goes well, I will finish it in about six months. This work is the second volume of *The First-Person Dilogy,* with *Sebastian in a Dream* being the first.

I don't remember how the first novel came about. Perhaps it stemmed from the need to write something personal, which prompted the name "The First-Person Dilogy," because both the first and the second novels are written in the first person POV, meaning "I." It was directly inspired by my short story "Father" from the collection *Short Tails*, which was influenced by Beckett's writing style. I decided to experiment with his form of internal monologue, and it turned into something of my own—I will make a certain statement and then contradict it, saying that it's not true, creating tension between what was said earlier and what is being said now. I really enjoy it—this uncertainty of what has been said, the struggle between truth and falsehood, which adds dynamism to the work. I use this technique in both novels of the dilogy.

Now about *Sebastian.* One of my favorite poets is Georg Trakl. It so happens that he was born on February 3rd, the same as me, although many years earlier. In addition, his first name is the same as mine (Georg is Yuriy in Ukrainian), and the first three letters of our last names are the same: "tar" and "tra." It's a remarkable coincidence, and it's one of the reasons why Trakl is dear to me. The second reason, and much more important one, is his poetry, which I find deeply harmonious. *"Sebastian im Traum,"* which is the original of "Sebastian in a dream," is one of Trakl's best poems, and I really love it. I used the first three lines of this poem as a motif for my novel—"Mother carried the child in a white moon." They have a double meaning—how she carried the child, whether in her womb or in arms, and what was moon—the moon or month. I wrote the entire work, based on this motif, incorporating details from my personal life, my biography. But monologues are formless, and I love form, so I structured the novel on one of my favorite works of Bach, *Goldberg Variations.* The same as the Bach composition, the novel consists of thirty variations, which are preceded and followed by an aria. But Bach developed his variations on musical basis, while I had to develop my own, which is extremely complicated, and I won't go into it here.

When I finished this novel, though, I still felt that I hadn't said everything I wanted to say, and for some reason, kept thinking about a man who lives alone in Toledo. Then I remembered how much I love the El Greco's painting and that I saw it in Toledo, so I decided to link the second novel to it. In this work, I analyze the thirty figures we have in the painting. The number thirty is a complete coincidence, but it was there, and I took advantage of it to formally connect the two books. The second part of analyzing each portrait includes my associations with Spain, where I once lived. However, this work is not biographical. It is a work of fiction that incorporates autobiographical elements.

Is there hope for a Ukrainian translation?

I don't know. But I certainly won't be doing it myself. I was lucky that I was able to work on the translation of my novel *Warm Arctic Nights* with Maxym Nestelieiev. He pretty much let me have a say on the vocabulary we used (for example, I didn't want to use the word *"soldat"* and we used *"vojak"* instead), which led to a very pure, natural Ukrainian. If I had written it myself, it would have turned out to be in a somewhat diasporan language, but this one is organically Ukrainian, with no trace of Russification. I am very satisfied with the translation, and am grateful to Tempora for publishing it, even though it apparently hasn't gotten much attention. This surprises me, because, as far as I know, it's the only novel describing World War II in Western Ukraine and the escape to the West. There were some Soviet literary works dealing with the war, but nothing about what happened in Western Ukraine and how people were escaping to the West.

-

By the way, in that interview in *The Collidescope*, George Salis asks me if I feel guilty for no longer writing in Ukrainian, and I say that I find it very comfortable to write in English, but that I am ready to switch to Ukrainian the moment a need for me to do it comes up. It looks like there isn't one coming any time soon. In other words, all is fine here, and I am perfectly satisfied with the state of affairs.

Yuriy Tarnawsky

Writers are often told that they should not be experts in all matters and should refrain from commenting on, for example, political events or other areas where they don't have a PhD. However, in our culture, the author has always been more than just a producer of texts, and personal experience is inherently significant. How do you feel about this? What is your definition of a writer?

I think you know what I'm going to say. To me, being a writer is a purely personal matter. It's not a profession, it's not a choice. It's a state. When you become a father, you are like a father—you have certain responsibilities, perform certain functions, act in certain ways. For me, being a writer is like being a father, with literature having taken place of the child.

I have said this many times before, but I'll say it again—it's not good for a poet to take on the role of a politician. Such people almost invariably turn out to be bad poets and bad politicians. If you are a poet, a writer, be that. To be a politician, you have to be born a politician. It rarely happens that there are both in one person. The two talents don't go together, and the flaws are always bound to come out.

First published in Craft Magazine, *June 19, 2023.*

Oleksandr Mymuk is a Ukrainian writer and editor.

A Checklist of JEF Titles
* Winners of the Kenneth Patchen Award for the Innovative Novel

www.ingramcontent.com/pod-product-compliance
Lightning Source LLC
Chambersburg PA
CBHW050759250626
47155CB00005B/2138